Seeing through Spiritual Eyes

Seeing through Spiritual Eyes

Expand Your View of Spiritual Reality,
Uncover the Mystery of Spiritual Warfare,
Envision the Path of Spiritual Well-Being

KIRK E. FARNSWORTH

WIPF & STOCK · Eugene, Oregon

SEEING THROUGH SPIRITUAL EYES
Expand Your View of Spiritual Reality, Uncover the Mystery of Spiritual
Warfare, Envision the Path of Spiritual Well-Being

Copyright © 2014 Kirk E. Farnsworth. All rights reserved. Except for brief
quotations in critical publications or reviews, no part of this book may
be reproduced in any manner without prior written permission from the
publisher. Write: Permissions, Wipf and Stock Publishers, 199 W. 8th Ave.,
Suite 3, Eugene, OR 97401.

Unless otherwise indicated, all Scripture quotations are taken from The
Holy Bible, New International Version®, NIV® Copyright © 1973, 1978,
1984 by Biblica, Inc.™ Used by permission. All rights reserved worldwide.

Wipf & Stock
An imprint of Wipf and Stock Publishers
199 W. 8th Ave., Suite 3
Eugene, OR 97401

www.wipfandstock.com

ISBN 13: 978-1-62564-831-0

Manufactured in the U.S.A.   09/16/2014

To Rosie

*Ordained minister
and
extraordinary mate and mom*

Contents

Illustrations | viii
Acknowledgments | ix
Foreword | xi
Introduction | xiii

PART I Winning the Battle
1   Spiritual Perspective | 3
2   Unsanctified Self | 8
3   Church Conflict | 13
4   Redemptive Memory | 23
5   Restoring Peace | 30

PART II Winning the War
6   Toxic Memories | 41
7   Spiritual Well-Being I | 52
8   Spiritual Well-Being II | 66
9   Meaningful Memories I | 75
10 Meaningful Memories II | 84

Afterword | 95
Appendix: Key Insights into Spiritual Warfare and Spiritual Welfare | 99
Bibliography | 103

Illustrations

Three Models for Restoration and Reconciliation | 32

Three Models for Power and Permanence | 33

Acknowledgments

I AM GRATEFUL THAT Wipf and Stock is the publisher of this book. For one thing, manuscripts are accepted for publication on merit, not on the projected market. For another, the focus is on the full scope of academic disciplines and church ministries. I have found a publishing home for my abiding interests of integrating psychology and theology, finding peace in church conflict, and embracing spiritual well-being.

Throughout the publishing process there was a cultural emphasis on excellence, good stewardship of resources, and a refreshing attitude of partnership in publisher-author relations. The latter was evident in the good working relationship among myself, my attentive-to-detail and reasonable editor, Matthew Wimer, and Kimberly Shoff, my good-natured and dependable typist who enthusiastically mastered the complexities of the many alterations of the original manuscript with computer skills beyond my imagination.

Foreword

The Author of the Bible is writing *us* into *his* book,
we aren't writing *him* into *ours*....
Our task is to obey, believingly, trustingly obey. Simply obey.

—Eugene H. Peterson[1]

How blessed is everyone who fears the Lord,
who walks in His ways....
You will be happy and it will be well with you.

—Psalm 128:1–2, NASB

I believe in Christianity [Christian spiritual reality] as I believe that the sun has risen, not only because I see it, but because by it, I see everything else.

—C.S. Lewis[2]

Do you have eyes but fail to see . . . ?

—Jesus (Mark 8:18a)

    1. Peterson, *Long Obedience*, 206.
    2. Lewis, "Is Theology Poetry?" 22.

Introduction

HAVE YOU EVER WISHED for a trouble-free life? Do you ever fancy acquiring peace regardless of the cost? Surely peace is what we all crave: peace with God, with neighbors, and within ourselves. We'll do almost anything to get it—some will even go to war if they have to. When conflict erupts in our families, on our jobs, or in our churches, when relationships get strained and we can't get back on track right away, our natural tendency is to ask, "Can't we just stop the fighting, get along with one another, and move one?" If that were to work, we would probably end up with something that looks like peace but that would not run very deep or last very long.

There are many possible reasons not to settle for what can rightly be referred to as pseudo-peace, that is, the appearance of peace (or absence of war), where we say, "'Peace, peace,' but there is no peace."[3] What we really should want is peace that is longstanding and unrestricted by a limited, self-serving perception of reality. What is too often left out of any discussion of human conflict in families, the workplace, and churches, and even within ourselves is an attempt to understand the spiritual reality of the situation.

The biblical record gives us every reason to suspect that any serious human conflict that does not involve the possible role of spiritual reality in the discussion of the problem and/or the

---

3. Jer 6:14, NASB.

solution will not likely lead to real, long-lasting peace. We need to reverse the modern tendency to marginalize evil and trivialize Satan. Wouldn't it be nice if we could get a handle on how Satan actually operates in human conflict, and how we personally participate in the process?

In the following chapters, I will attempt to answer the following questions:

1. Can we expose the human factors that Satan uses and connect them with how he uses them?

2. Can we produce objective evidence of a battle within one's inner self that will provide a deeper understanding of the reality of demonic influence in the life of believers?

3. Can we find a biblical approach that puts an end to troublemakers being personal conduits for demonic influence in church conflict and that resolves the conflict—instead of fleeing, faking it, or fighting back?

4. Can we find a biblical approach to put an end to the prolonged suffering of victims from toxic memories from their painful past?

5. Can we move past finding peace in the midst of and in the memories of traumatic events to the in-between times of ordinary everyday life?

6. Can we develop a strong sense of spiritual well-being and a memory bank of sanctified, meaningful memories?

I believe we can win both the battle and the war. We can connect church conflict and satanic influences and successfully fight our "personal demons." We can peacefully manage poisoned relationships and other collateral damage. We can claim victory in Christ by bringing our sinful attitudes and actions, as well as our toxic memories burned into us by the conflict, under the lordship of Christ. And as a pathway for finding lasting peace, developing spiritual well-being, and creating meaningful memories, I have gathered up all these concerns into a list of "Key Insights into

Spiritual Warfare and Spiritual Welfare" in the appendix at the end of this book.

But we can win both the battle and the war and still lose the peace. One of the main contributions of this book is to move beyond the preservation of the physical, psychological, and spiritual wholeness of our being in the context of spiritual conflict. We must focus especially on our spiritual well-being, the holiness of our being, in the context of our progressive sanctification into Christlikeness.

In many ways, this book is a companion to and an extension of my book *When the Bride Is Attacked*. At the end of that book is a brief essay on the problem of evil. I introduce it with these words:

> We must remember that evil is absolutely the most serious problem that could occur in any conflict. Satan will use conflict every chance he gets. This does not mean that every conflict is evil. It does mean that there is no more fertile ground for satanic activity. Conflict brings with it an untold number of openings for Satan to establish footholds in people to distort the conflict for his own diabolical purposes. What more effective way could he possibly use to bring down a strong, healthy church?[4]

I am sounding the trumpet about the marginalizing of evil. Almost without exception, today's healthy churches do not expect to see spiritual conflict in any material way at any time in their future, and churches in conflict do not seriously consider the possibility of spiritual conflict even when it breaks out in their midst. Just because they don't anticipate it or recognize it does not mean that Satan is not the single most powerful threat to their very existence.

The postmodern approach to resolving church conflict is to recognize that everyone has a share in the blame and must repent to restore an equal-footing balance, or peace through reconciliation. All sins are assumed to be equal, and evil is marginalized as the bad side of human nature. It's reduced to a psychological issue, devoid of actual demonic influence. The spiritual issue is confined

---

4. Farnsworth, *When the Bride* Is Attacked, 143–44.

Introduction

to how the Holy Spirit can heal, and does not take into account how Satan can hurt. The fact is, both the Spirit and Satan, from the spiritual realm, can materially impact in the earthly realm the course of unhealthy church conflict.

Most approaches to peacemaking (in the generic sense, without reference to a specific method) skirt the issue of the objective spiritual reality of evil. We read statements such as, "Remember that often the evil in our desires is not in what we want but in the fact that we want it too much."[5] Overlooked is the fact that often it is also Satan himself who is the evil in our desires! His footprints are all over our hard-hearted, mean-spirited, self-serving tantrums to get our own way.

This is a fatal flaw in popular thinking. Yes, we must face *why* we desire so desperately things we cannot have, but we must also face *what* it is we must have and *how* we go about getting it. Rather than casting aside the objective presenting issue (what we want) in favor of the "real" issue (why we want it so badly), we must recognize that often the real issue is what Satan fervently wants and how he is going about getting it. That is precisely how evil is often manifested in unhealthy church conflict: Satan's desires masked as ours.

Evil must be dealt with up front and directly. Peacemaking must be first and foremost a matter of righteousness. Spiritual conflict must be combatted with discipline of rebellious behavior and deliverance from demonic influence. Righteousness therefore precedes reconciliation. Righteousness is the foundation; reconciliation is the fruit. Nowhere in the Bible is it suggested that we should dine with the devil by reconciling good and evil, God and Satan!

On a more personal note, as I was developing the material for this book, I was deeply moved by former pastors and devoted church members, all of whom had not yet—years later—recovered from devastating church conflict. There was a common sense of being victims of ruthless rebellion and even bullying. They seemed emotionally spent, mentally worn out, and spiritually confused.

---

5. Barthel and Edling, *Redeeming Church Conflicts*, 69.

Introduction

They were wandering through space half-heartedly hoping to bump into an answer. Closure. Closeness to God. Relief from bondage to toxic memories.

I suggested to these people that they might consider the healing power of the inspirational stories recorded in redemptive biblical history. I recommended one story in particular: the Joseph story.[6] Here we have the well-known story about young Joseph being sold into slavery by his brothers, followed by a prolonged and difficult journey toward reconciliation. In between is Joseph's profound, life-changing statement, "God has made me forget."[7] Why couldn't that happen to them too?

One of the pastors told me later that he took my advice. He said he let Joseph's words fully occupy his thoughts, and the Holy Spirit gradually made him forget the toxic memories he had been in bondage to for so long. "I am Joseph," he exclaimed with pure joy. "Of course God made me forget. He created the heavens and earth just by speaking them into existence. If he could make me in the first place, he most certainly could make me forget those horrible memories!"

I don't want this to sound like presumptive faith—assuming that God will act just the way we expect him to act, in some "magical" way. Scripture does not lay out the details of Joseph's act of forgetting. I can only assume there was a gradual process of drawing near to God and being faithful in his walk that led to Joseph's actual forgetting. And I don't think any particular time frame is the issue.

This book will help you make Joseph's story your own. There's a certain amount of sanctifying prayer and preparatory memory work, however, that must be done. It is all part of the spiritual pathway of our faithful walk with the Lord. It is the Spirit-formed well-being of staying on course rather than straying off course. In short, it is delighting in seeing God at work and being involved in what he is doing.

---

6. See Gen 37–50.
7. Gen 41:51.

Introduction

The rest of the story of embracing spiritual well-*being* is enhancing the meaningfulness of what we are *doing*, that is, finding peace plus finding meaning. The final two chapters of this book are an integration of biblical faith and the exciting new scientific field of brain research into the creative process of making meaning. It's not science versus faith. It's not brain versus Bible! It's about God being directly involved at the very center of a science-based, Spirit-guided search for meaning in every aspect of our daily lives. It's pretty fascinating stuff!

PART I

Winning the Battle

1

Spiritual Perspective

Jesus said, "If you hold to my teaching . . . you will know the truth, and the truth will set you free . . . you will be free indeed."[1] Really free. Free from bondage of sin, from captivity to Satan. Free to "soar on wings like eagles" with "hope in the Lord."[2] The love of Christ sets us free to be filled with the fullness of God.[3]

We can conclude that the sense of *truth* Jesus is referring to is not inactive truthful ideas, doctrines, or propositions, but rather the redeeming actions of God that are actually experienced—the *reality* of the "fullness of God." We could say that gospel truth is not just a message from God but the existential reality of the true nature of God—e.g., the reality of God's peace in the midst of conflict.[4]

So what is "captivity to Satan" all about? How real is it, and what can we do about it? What we have to do first is recognize the presence and potency of spiritual realities alongside the presence and potency of physical and psychological realities. Second, we have

---

1. John 8:31–36.
2. Isa 40:31.
3. See Eph 3:19.
4. This congruence between faith and reality borrows from Myers, *Eerdmans Bible Dictionary*, 1022.

PART I—Winning the Battle

to ask the question, how do the spiritual realities of the Holy Spirit and Satan operate in the world we live in? Let's look more closely at the importance of recognizing spiritual reality, and at two specific areas of human endeavor working alongside spiritual activity: converting spiritual conflict and building spiritual well-being.

SPIRITUAL REALITY

Scripture anticipates that as fully devoted followers of Jesus we will experience the spiritual reality of the fullness of God. Likewise, we will experience the spiritual reality of the destructiveness of Satan. Jesus himself experienced spiritual realities all the way from communing with the Father to casting out demons. What we need are credible ways of assessing and identifying these realities that are often beyond measure but are knowable and true. Using Scripture as our guide, we can and must be aware of the multitude of ways that the Holy Spirit will heal us and Satan will hurt us in the course of our everyday living.

The trouble is, when we think about spiritual reality, we often truncate our thoughts with the caution not to spiritualize our troubles away. We correctly tell ourselves not to take false comfort in the hope that Jesus will fix everything to make us feel better, and not to see a demon under every rock so we can avoid personal responsibility for our own actions. However, we can try too hard to exclude certain kinds of spiritual reality—keep the spiritual world "in its place"—by turning a blind eye and missing the truth of what is actually going on.

The very nature of Jesus—fully divine and fully human—as well as the testimony about his life throughout Scripture, give credence to quite the opposite view of spiritual reality. The nature and life of Jesus simply do not allow us to get away with bifurcating reality into two unrelated realms of earthly and heavenly, seen and unseen, objective and subjective. He will not let us get away with that. We also have the testimony of the two realities operating in our personal experience of salvation, whereby we ask Jesus into our heart and receive the heavenly activity of the Holy Spirit in our earthly inner self. The two realities are undeniably compatible and coexistent with each other. The lines are blurred between these dual realities that are present at every moment every day of our lives. In other words, earthly and heavenly realities thoroughly commingle across seamless shared boundaries.

As we shall see later in this book, a major factor in discerning spiritual reality is our ability to imagine what it looks like. Imagination is key to getting it right. But our picture of spiritual reality can easily be clouded by the cataracts of a limited imagination. When we don't see accurately because our imagination is biased, restrained, or inactive, we will be much less likely to get it right.

SPIRITUAL CONFLICT

Satan (referred to as the *author* of confusion and disorder and not of peace[5]) is at work all around us, all the time. God is also at work all around us, all the time. They are the primary spiritual actors in both earthly and heavenly realities. Satan is a fallen angel and cannot do anything God does not allow him to do. God is Spirit, referred to in the Bible as Father, Son, and Holy Spirit—same in essence, different in expression—and as being in ultimate control over both realms of reality. It is safe to conclude that we can and should address spiritual realities. We must not avoid them! The Bible says that sin is crouching at our door, eager to pounce and devour us.[6] But we are also reassured that he who lives in us is greater than he who is in the world.[7]

Spiritual conflict, pure and simple, is real. We must live every day in the midst of the battle, and we must do so with faith, not fear. That is the choice that Jesus, who exposed and defeated Satan on the cross, made possible for us to choose. Indeed, he won the victory, and what we must do is claim the victory. Jesus also went so far as to give us earth-bound human beings *authority* over

---

5. See 1 Cor 14:33.
6. See Gen 4:7.
7. See 1 John 4:4.

demonic spiritual beings as well as authority to heal diseases in the earthly realm. That's a fact. He gave his disciples power and authority over demons and diseases.[8] He bestowed upon those who believe authority over demons and the power to make well those who are sick.[9] Biblical authority is power and influence, command and control. Satan may be the author, but we have the authority!

Where there are opposite powers, there is bound to be conflict. We must consider the spiritual reality of conflict between them. I am well aware, however, that many thoughtful, devoted Christians are uncomfortable with the phrase "spiritual warfare" and are wary or dismissive of its reality in their own lives. Hopefully "spiritual conflict" will be more acceptable and helpful for them. I am using this phrase to refer to the spiritual battles we personally encounter that are more limited in scope and targeted in focus than the all-encompassing scope and long-lasting effects of spiritual war between the forces of good and evil. My goal is to provide a clearer picture of the various forms of inner conflict that are actually involved: mental conflict, emotional conflict, and spiritual conflict.

The real battleground is the inner self, where demonic influence meets up with the power of the Holy Spirit, and our personal attitudes and actions have to face the conviction of the Holy Spirit. Spiritual conflict is not one-directional (fighting the enemy) but two-directional (outward battle with the enemy plus inward struggle with one's own sinful thoughts, feelings, and behaviors). Spiritual warfare is not a misnomer, however; it refers in this book to long-term unresolved combat and struggle, including many battles at not only the individual but also the institutional and national levels. It also applies to intractable battles/struggles that are kept alive for months and years by toxic memories of the painful past.

SPIRITUAL WELL-BEING

I am taking the spiritual high ground. I am transitioning from arming people for spiritual warfare to concern for their spiritual

8. See Luke 9:1.
9. See Mark 16:17–18.

welfare (well-being and happiness, in addition to dealing with adversity). And, recognizing that either management or resolution of conflict can be a positive outcome, I am testifying that claiming victory in Jesus over the powers of darkness is the source of spiritual well-being in both the management and the resolution of spiritual conflict.

Because of Jesus, we have the blessed assurance that victory is his, not Satan's. We can joyfully submit to and rest in Jesus, rather than fearfully deny Satan's powers and unknowingly suffer the consequences. In the words of Fanny Crosby's wonderful old hymn, "Blessed assurance, Jesus is mine! . . . Filled with His goodness, lost in His love. This is my story, this is my song, praising my Savior all the day long."[10] And again, "Jesus will guard His children; in His arms He carries them all day long. Praise Him! Praise Him! Tell of His excellent greatness! Praise Him! Praise Him! Ever in joyful song!"[11]

Because of Jesus, we can live with rock-solid faith every day, "all day long," and unwaveringly find lasting peace in the midst of the battle and beyond. *First*, we must understand that spiritual conflict is undeniable and a normal part of the Christian life. *Second*, it is important that we understand how Satan works to personally influence our lives and through us the lives of other believers, and how the Holy Spirit works within us so that we can claim victory in Jesus. *Third*, we need to understand that winning the battle must lead to winning the war: finding lasting peace by forgetting the toxic memories from our painful past that continue to haunt us for months and years, regardless of whether the battle was won or lost. *Finally*, we must understand that "final" peace is not decided ultimately by winning the war. Winning the peace, however, through Spirit-formed well-being and meaningful memories, will move us significantly in the direction of both final peace in the form of reconciliation and ultimate well-being in the form of rest.

---

10. Crosby, "Blessed Assurance."
11. Crosby, "Praise Him! Praise Him!"

2

Unsanctified Self

A MAJOR ACCOMPLISHMENT OF this book will be to bring the otherworldly mystery of spiritual conflict down to earth by making an objective connection between human dynamics and spiritual forces. For starters, here's how Satan gets things going:

1. Spiritual conflict begins the moment you accept Jesus.
2. As you grow as a Christian, it is normal for Satan to target you for that reason.
3. Satan notices when you put on the full armor of God as a fully devoted follower of Jesus.
4. Then Satan looks for any cracks in the armor that you have not brought under the lordship of Jesus Christ that open doors for Satan to create footholds of demonic influence.
5. Finally, Satan uses what you give him to take you captive to do his will.[1]

This places the real battle in the inner self, where the fire of the Spirit (our God is a consuming fire[2]) and the depravity of Satan

---

1. See 2 Tim 2:26.
2. See Deut 4:24; Heb 12:29.

collide. What we see on the outside is how the demonic influences manifest themselves in real, observable human behavior. So our *first job* is to establish the biblical reality/truth of what we see. Our *second job* is to match these outward behaviors with the cracks in our armor—sinful ways—that have not yet been yielded to the Spirit. The evidence of demonic influence is the similarities of the behavioral manifestations of demonic influence and the behavioral expressions of our sinful ways, with a notable increase in both intensity and destructiveness.

Spiritual conflict is grounded in real, objective human experience. I believe the most obvious connection between Satan's activity and human affairs is unsanctified thoughts, feelings, actions, and memories. They become his, masked as ours. They create a multitude of openings for Satan to use for his own diabolical purposes.

Consider the fact that as Christians we are fully redeemed but not fully sanctified. In other words, we are bought and paid for in full, but we still have aspects of our lives that have not yet been brought under the lordship of Jesus Christ.

We must also consider the important role that the unsanctified self plays in Satan's entry into an individual's life and the life of the church. Both Tom White in his book *Breaking Strongholds*, and E. Stanley Jones in his book *A Song of Ascents*, refer to a similar concept—a place in the human psyche where painful issues and deep layers of hurt connected to traumatic memories, unresolved broken relationships, and fearful anticipation of the future remain unyielded to the Spirit. According to Jones, they remain unsurrendered, outside of conscious awareness, and are typically recognizable only by their behavioral effects. Subconscious material can be pretty messy. Jones warns us: "Touch it and it will blow its top."[3] And when Satan gets into the mix, White advises us: "We can shut the door on supernatural aggravation of our natural vulnerabilities *primarily* by submitting to God and his truth. Resisting Satan's manipulation and exploitation of our selfishness is secondary."[4] In

---

3. Jones, *Victory through Surrender*, 92.
4. White, *Breaking Strongholds*, 41.

other words, when God's word is spoken, our self-will is broken, and it shuts the liar's mouth!

I do not restrict the unsanctified self exclusively to the subconscious. It is obvious that not all our disturbing thoughts and negative emotions are outside of conscious awareness. Conscious material also brings a lot of baggage to the battle: such as trauma from an abusive childhood situation, threat of the exposure of a secret sin, or agony over an addiction and its physical, emotional, and relational effects. We want to get even or blame or deny. The battle is with our conscience: do it versus don't do it. Or sometimes our conscience is subdued, locked away subconsciously. Then we allow ourselves to do what we want without hesitation, if it satisfies our selfish desires, e.g., unforgiveness, deception, acts of rebellion.

The most important takeaway from all this is that, subconscious or conscious, we need to observe our objective behavior to get a handle on the nature of the real battlefield of spiritual conflict. And it is there, in the unsanctified self, that healing and sanctification take place and spiritual conflict comes to an end.

In the meantime, heightened mental and emotional turmoil is sure to get Satan's attention. Evil thoughts, feelings, and actions are right up his alley. And when he acts, the battle is on. The battle now is with Satan. The evidence of the battle between satanic influence and human choice is behavioral manifestations that are unmistakably corrupt and depraved. The behaviors fit the person but are more extreme and destructive. Scripture gives support for what I am talking about and pretty much sums up the rest of the story. It says that if you harbor bitter envy and selfish ambition in your heart, Satan will enter in and turn them into disorder and all sorts of evil practices. It all starts when you want something and can't get it, so your desires battle within you. You quarrel and fight. Your selfish desires cannot be met, so you act out your inner turmoil by inflicting pain on others. You must resist the devil. Come near to God and he will come near to you. Purify your heart, and he will lift you up.[5] Notice that spiritual conflict starts and ends in the inner self. Satan uses your selfish desires to cause rebellion and

---

5. See Jas 3:14–16; 4:1–2, 7–8, 10.

every evil practice. You must resist him by coming near to God so that the Holy Spirit can purify your heart. And he will lift you up. This spiritual battle is over.

That's the good news. The bad news is when we don't draw near to God and allow the Holy Spirit to enter our innermost parts to do the work we so desperately need. Essentially, by failing to sanctify the unsanctified aspects of our inner life, we give Satan—in Francis Frangipane's words—access to our secret resentments and unresolved issues, which he can use to fulfill every demonic gratification.[6] We fall into the trap of the devil, who has taken us captive to do his will. We are being held captive in the battle within—fighting our own demons (demons from whom we are under personal attack). Tragically, we began with selfish gratification and have ended up with demonic gratification!

Rebecca Nichols Alonzo's recent best-selling book *The Devil in Pew Number Seven* is a powerful account of how evil the trap of the devil can get. It vividly portrays one man's extreme bullying of his pastor. Unfortunately, "the devil" is used only as a metaphor to describe the "disturbing individual with deep psychological issues" sitting in pew number seven. Spiritual conflict as such is not part of the author's analysis. On the other hand, the record of that man's evil deeds toward the pastor and his family and the resulting lifelong suffering of the author and her brother is a gut-wrenching tour de force that substantiates some important points in this book:

- Remembering must be done truthfully.
- Forgetting depends on justice, however long it takes.
- Forgiving is necessary but not enough.
- Finding peace is a daily battle within oneself—"I wanted to forget. I wanted to remember. I had difficulty doing either. A tug-of-war between equally compelling needs raged within me."[7]

---

6. Frangipane, *House United*, 128.
7. Alonzo, *Pew Number Seven*, 207.

PART I—Winning the Battle

- Reconciling is the final step for final peace, even "from a distance if necessary."

Let's take a closer look at these important aspects of spiritual conflict: remembering, forgetting, forgiving, finding peace, and reconciling. But *first*, we must establish through objective analysis how the inner personal life of a single individual can become outwardly disruptive behavior that can ultimately poison the entire church. *Second*, we will undertake an objective analysis of how Satan uses what people give him to manufacture and magnify conflict that can ultimately kill the bride of Christ.

3
Church Conflict

How does the power of darkness[1] manifest Satan's presence in the life of the church? How do we recognize it? White lists some helpful objective marks of a church under satanic attack:

- A person or persons who inject bitterness, strife or rebellion against authority into the everyday life of the church
- A battle for control of church governance
- A distinct deadness and pervasive non-responsiveness in worship services
- A cloud of confusion hanging over the congregation[2]

This is not a complete list of all the different aspects of spiritual conflict in the church, but when we see some of these things come to the surface—most likely accompanied by disregard for church order and civility, to obtain personal desires—we must take notice.

What we see can range anywhere from frivolous to flagrant, from trivial personal preferences all the way to outright

---

1. See Luke 22:52–53.
2. White, *Breaking Strongholds*, 124–25.

conspiracies led by "noisy gangs of evil-doers," whose actions are readily apparent:

- They "aim poisoned words like arrows."
- "They shoot unexpectedly and without self-restraint."
- "They confirm for themselves an evil agreement."
- "They talk of laying snares secretly."
- "They work out wicked schemes."
- "They are ready with a well-conceived plan."[3]

When other, trustworthy people begin to say things like "That's from the pit" and "This is spiritual warfare," especially when said by someone with the gift of discernment of spirits, it's time to seriously consider that it is. I acknowledge how difficult that can be, especially when the troublemakers are respected members of the congregation and personal friends. Because of these important factors, especially in the context of church conflict, we must make sure that we're talking about publicly observable and verifiable events with legitimately perceptible meanings. We must not interject agendas or impute motives.

TAKING OFFENSE AND SOWING DISCORD

What we are dealing with here is understanding how the inner personal life of someone becomes outwardly disruptive behavior that affects others in the church. The most common unsanctified action, and perhaps the most effective of all the weapons at Satan's disposal that emerges from the battle within the unsanctified self, is taking offense. This is a judgmental attitude toward someone else's so-called faults, weaknesses, or wrongdoing that often leads to making a list of perceived offenses and harboring escalating, unresolved anger. In its most infectious form it is taking on the offenses of others—triangulating—by engaging in the

---

3. See Psalm 64:2–6, Berkeley.

sin of gossip rather than prompting the two parties in conflict to communicate directly.

Unresolved anger leads to malice (gossip), which leads to slander (calling names), which leads to self-righteous contempt, which leads to condemnation. This is the lockstep progression of sin outlined by Jesus in the Sermon on the Mount. It is also rebuked by Paul: when angry, don't sin; leave no room or foothold for Satan; let all bitterness and indignation be banished from you.[4] That's the theology of it. Here's the psychology of it, taken from Dallas Willard's award-winning book *The Divine Conspiracy*:

> Anger indulged always has in it an element of self-righteousness and a wounded ego. The importance of the self and the real or imaginary wound done to it is blown out of all proportion. Then anger can become anything from a low-burning resentment to a holy crusade to inflict harm on the one who has thwarted me or my wishes.[5]

Taking offense and unresolved anger are natural preconditions for rebellion or sowing discord, which is at the center of most unhealthy church conflicts. Of all that the Lord hates, sowing discord is the worst. In the Old Testament we find six things the Lord hates—no, seven: pride, lying, needless killing, wicked thoughts, plotting evil, false witness—and sowing discord.[6] This is not just a list of seven reprehensible sins. One stands out from the rest, as clearly explained by R. Laird Harris in *The Wycliffe Bible Commentary*: "These are not seven cardinal sins nor an indefinite six or seven. . . . [Rather,] the proverb is climactic. The six items are background for the seventh, which receives the emphasis (cf. Job 5:19; Prov. 30:18–19). The statement emphatically concludes with what verse 14 had introduced—'letting loose strife'"[7] (i.e., sowing discord).

---

4. See Eph 4:26–31.
5. Willard, *Divine Conspiracy*, 149.
6. See Prov 6:16–19.
7. Harris, "Proverbs," 563.

In its most extreme form rebellion is called, in Guy Greenfield's words, pathological antagonism.[8] I call it toxic obstructionism, a fight compulsively looking for somewhere to happen. Scripture makes similar reference to a morbid craving for controversy stemming from envy, bad suspicions, and perpetual contention.[9]

It is very important that we recognize the seriousness of taking offense and rebellion over other more minor sins. Not all sins are equal. Under the influence of our postmodern culture, however, many Christians have watered down evil through a philosophical commitment to moral equivalence. Miroslav Volf in his award-winning book *Exclusion and Embrace* gives wise counsel: "From 'All are sinners' *it does not follow* that 'All sins are equal;' from 'Neither is innocent' one cannot conclude 'The sins of both are equal.' . . . The equality of sins dissolves all concrete sins in an ocean of undifferentiated sinfulness. This is precisely what the prophets and Jesus did not do."[10] And they also most certainly did not marginalize evil as an otherworldly metaphor rather than an objective reality in human affairs!

COPING MECHANISMS

Just how is it that a battle within the self morphs into a battle within the church? What are the psychological dynamics of being quick to take offense and sowing discord, and spiritual conflict in the church?

A fruitful theoretical framework for our understanding is family systems theory. Church members are simultaneously involved in their own family systems and the church family system. This creates an emotional interface between individual families and the church family as a whole that provides a potent context for the inevitability of church conflict.

---

8. Greenfield, *Wounded Minister*, 35–45.
9. See 1 Tim 6:4–5.
10. Volf, *Exclusion and Embrace*, 82.

Displacement. The church becomes a receptacle for the displacement of important unresolved family issues, says Rabbi Edwin Friedman, who has done seminal work in applying family systems theory to churches and synagogues.[11] We act at church like we act at home, as the church becomes a dumping ground for relieving the anxiety, anger, hurt, and/or shame from things like financial difficulties, divorce, unresolved issues between a parent and his or her own parents, juvenile delinquency, and/or, most especially, besetting (constant, long-term) sin. Simply put, displacement is a psychological coping mechanism for shifting all that negative emotion onto an issue or person(s) at church—real or imagined—and in extreme cases turning it into a holy crusade.

Friedman cautions that when people complain about their pastor's performance, there's a good chance they are displacing something from their own personal lives. There's also a good chance that the emotional intensity of the conflict is really a reflection of disruptive behavioral patterns learned in dysfunctional families being acted out in the church. More than likely, the destructive potential for the church lies not in the issue(s) per se but rather in the harmful emotional processes going on in the family/families who are most actively promoting the conflict and bringing such disruptive things into the life of the church. The inflammatory power brought to the conflict, Friedman concludes, is usually caused by those family members assuming that it is the issue that created the problem, overlooking the real, personal cause of their misery by focusing on the object of their discontent.

Transference. A second psychological coping mechanism is called transference. This one fills in the details of displacement and helps explain the emotional intensity that causes unhealthy conflict, where concerns become convulsions and rational discourse turns into irrational displays of negative emotions. Transference refers to repressed painful memories from unresolved personal problems or a past abusive relationship, which are transferred into a present relationship. It is an unconscious process of creating an interpersonal situation that resembles a traumatic reality in the

---

11. See Friedman, *Generation to Generation.*

past and acting it out in ways that reshape and distort the consciously perceived reality of the present relationship.

Transference in the church typically starts out as a petty, exaggerated complaint (taking offense) against an authority figure, most often the pastor. Such grievances come from an irrational and intense emotional reaction to something in the present that is unconsciously connected to emotional trauma from the past. Because of the unconscious connection between the past and the present (e.g., rage against an unloving parent and intense anger at a perceived lack of compassion by the parent-figure pastor), the present relationship will become a battleground for resolving the emotional pain from the past. The stage is set for the built-up emotional force of the transference to become an illusional obsession that avoids resolving the real conflict with the parent and acknowledging the delusional attitudes and sinful actions toward the pastor.

Self-deception. The stage is also set for sowing discord throughout the congregation. This is where a third psychological coping mechanism comes in: self-deception. This is recasting unresolved anger as okay, while justifying disrespectful, uncivil, harmful behavior because of the "goodness of the cause." In addition, it is self-righteous disregard for truth and biblical warnings about the consequences of one's actions. Then, because there will always be other members of the congregation who have their own misgivings about the pastor—real or imagined—there will be people who can be targeted and recruited to join the conflict "for the good of the church."

Rallying around a "good cause" as part of a rebellious group is, as Gregg Ten Elshof warns in his book *I Told Me So*, actually a commitment to an unrighteous cause and is more than likely dead to the moral value of anything or anyone perceived as standing in the way. This is a powerful picture of the self-deception of groupthink. Victims of groupthink are seduced into thinking that if they join forces, just about anything they do is justified because of the mutually perceived goodness of their cause. Ten Elshof concludes that "what would present itself as obvious and egregious disrespect and mistreatment if considered alone is granted moral legitimacy by the group consciousness in devotion to a cause."[12] That's dangerous stuff, especially when Satan gets his hands on it!

CONTROLLING SPIRITS

If we wish to truly understand satanic influence as an objective reality, our *first job* is to establish the biblical reality or truth of what we are talking about. Our *second job* is to match the biblical reality of controlling spirits and their behavioral manifestations with the objective reality of mismanaged personal problems and their publicly verifiable psychological coping mechanisms.

Let's unpack what I just said. I define spiritual conflict in terms of the interaction of a variety of mismanaged personal problems with satanic influence. I have presented the former in detail. What we bring to the table are unresolved painful memories, troublemaking behavioral patterns learned through dysfunctional family histories, pathological personality characteristics, and besetting sins that we mismanage and mask using psychological coping mechanisms.

Now let's deal with satanic influence, as we look at how Satan uses what we give him. I find it fascinating how our mismanaged personal problems and psychological coping mechanisms match up closely with the behavioral manifestations of the controlling spirits under Satan's control. I also find it interesting how taking offense and sowing discord in particular are exploited and escalated by Satan's influence and how our actions become *his*—masked as *ours*—as he manufactures, mobilizes, magnifies, and multiplies problems in the church. It's so subtle. When we give Satan an opening and he gains a foothold in our inner thoughts, he slowly magnifies them and makes them worse. We don't notice it, because they're our own thoughts. We're just doing our thing, thinking it's not a big deal and not noticing that it is getting worse and beginning to hurt other people. When it's called to our attention, we

---

12. Ten Elshof, *I Told Me So*, 93.

cannot believe it. We are actually doing what Satan wants us to do. His thoughts are our thoughts. We are confused, and guess what: Satan is also the author of confusion!

The most predominant biblical reality of satanic influence in human affairs is controlling spirits. Three stand out in church-based spiritual conflict: the spirit of Antichrist, the spirit of Absalom, and the spirit of Jezebel.

Spirit of Antichrist. The spirit of Antichrist is behind most church splits. It is a governing spirit that directs satanic attack against the church. We need not be confused by the Antichrist that will manifest in human form prior to Christ's return. Scripture describes this individual and also the nature of the Antichrist spirit in its invisible form.[13] Essentially, we're talking about hardness of heart, unforgiveness, and sowing discord.

People with the gift of discernment of spirits can sense the presence of the Antichrist spirit in an atmosphere that is filled with hollowness, in an aura of coldness and deadness that fills the room, and in the scowl on the faces of those under its influence. This is particularly evident in worship services in churches that have come under attack. But it does not mean that each person with a scowl on his or her face must be delivered from satanic influence!

Spirit of Absalom. The nature of the spirit of Absalom is revealed in the story of betrayal of King David by his son Absalom.[14] It's a story of taking offense, deception, and conspiracy. It is a prime example of rebellion against God's anointed leaders and is the biblical basis for the spirit of Absalom. The most telling mark of the Absalom spirit is sowing discord.

Fuchsia Pickett in her book *The Next Move of God* describes in detail how unresolved offenses can open up a person to the influence of the Absalom spirit through the development of spiritual pride and the belief that he is more spiritual than those in church leadership. This leads to misrepresenting decisions of the leadership and drawing a group of people to himself, who feed off his critical spirit. And it escalates from there into a bold conspiracy:

---

13. See 2 Thess 2; 1 John 2 and 4.
14. See 2 Sam 13:23—15:12.

justifying his group's actions through minor issues and accusations "not related to false doctrine or blatant sin within the leadership. Rather, he magnifies the imperfections or human traits of the leader."[15]

Taking offense and sowing discord are two major weapons of mass destruction in Satan's arsenal. But they are not *about* the problem; they *are* the problem. Perhaps the pastor rubs some people the wrong way—perhaps he's too "controlling." But the truth of the matter just might be that the troublemakers have misjudged the pastor's actions, when he is in fact simply trying to do the job God has given him to do!

Spirit of Jezebel. Like the spirit of Absalom, the spirit of Jezebel is self-promoting and consumed with desire for control and contempt for authority. Like pathological antagonists, it is vicious and arrogantly rebellious. This manifestation of the power of darkness takes its name from one of the most despicable persons in the Bible.

The story of the Jezebel spirit begins with Queen Jezebel, the deceptive and rebellious wife of King Ahab. She is first seen in Scripture killing off the Lord's prophets and inciting hundreds of false prophets. After additional nefarious adventures, this "cursed woman" dies a ghastly death.[16] She is also mentioned in the New Testament in the letter written to the church at Thyatira. Here we have a situation where the symbolic Jezebel is to the church at Thyatira what she was to her husband Ahab: idolatrous, immoral, and controlling through any and all means of seduction, deception, and domination.[17]

The strongest evidence of the influence of the Jezebel spirit is control—on steroids. It's so fierce that someone corrupted by this spirit yields to no one. Prophetic leader? Disparage and distort the true prophetic voice and counterfeit a prophetic anointing in yourself—like Jezebel, who *called herself* a prophetess.[18]

15. Pickett, *Next Move of God*, 59.
16. See 1 Kgs 16; 18–19; 21; 2 Kgs 9.
17. See Rev 2.
18. See Rev 2:20.

Prayer? Distract and derail intercessory prayer and devalue corporate prayer. Spiritual authority? Be divisive in matters of church governance and disdainful of the pastor's spiritual authority, in order to destroy him.

Rebel against any authority that disagrees with you. Recruit others to rebel against pastoral authority. "Meanwhile, church members who seem indifferent or complacent to this rebellion will end up serving as pawns in a demonic game of win or lose. Tragically, the end result will usually be a church split."[19]

---

19. Jackson, *Unmasking the Jezebel Spirit*, 122.

4

Redemptive Memory

SPIRITUAL CONFLICT IS ALWAYS present, all around us and within our selves—our unsanctified selves. Every person alive engages in an ongoing battle within oneself between good and evil. For Christians, it's a matter of dying to self, of yielding to the Spirit, of bringing all thoughts and feelings, actions and reactions under the lordship of Jesus Christ.

How do we bring the Holy Spirit into our personal battle within, where the fire of the Spirit and the depravity of Satan collide? An effective military strategy of warfare is to search and destroy—in this instance, search out demonic activity in the community and confront it with the name of Jesus and command the demon to go to the place that has been prepared for it.

I have previously written a book on confronting demonic attack in the church through corrective/restorative discipline corporately, while individually and biblically managing relationships with rebellious friends and finding peace in the midst of the battle.[1] That book focuses on the inner battle and is about prevention and intervention to block and stop being a personal conduit for demonic influence in unhealthy church conflict, with the result

---

1. Farnsworth, *When the Bride Is Attacked*.

being peace that lasts. Also, that book is about (a) researching the cause, (b) resolving the conflict, (c) recovering from the conflict, and (d) reframing the future. This book is about (e) restoring the inner self and (f) regenerating toxic memories.

Our strategy needs to be twofold. *First*, we need to focus on release from negative feelings from the past that are causing emotional problems in the present. This focuses on redemptive memory. Lewis Smedes in his book *Forgive and Forget* uses the example of the biblical history of the Jews to point out that God's intended blessing is in our release and redemption from the pain and suffering of the past. We will be blessed by the release of possibilities for the future if we are able to forget the emotional horrors of the past. "Redemptive memory is focused on love emerging from ashes, hope that survives remembered evil."[2]

The issue is how to "forget the emotional horrors" that accompany "remembered evil." Miroslav Volf helps by dividing the concept of redemptive memory into redemptive forgetting and redemptive remembering, or forgetting the feelings but not the facts (the emotions but not the events) of our painful past. He refers to a "certain kind of forgetting" that forgets the pain of the wound but not the fact of the wound. It is preventing the unwelcome resurfacing and intrusion of painful feelings from the past that upset the present.

REDEMPTIVE FORGETTING

This is implied in Scripture: "The former things shall not be remembered or come to mind"[3] and "Forget the former things; do not dwell on the past."[4] A powerful example is contained in the story of Joseph: "God has made me forget all my troubles and everyone in my father's family"[5]—in other words, all the misery caused

---

2. Smedes, *Forgive and Forget*, 137.
3. Isa 65:17, NASB.
4. Isa 43:18.
5. Gen 41:51, NLT.

by my brothers. That truly is a special kind of forgetting, a blessing straight from God! All the years of tears, all those toxic feelings gathered inside Joseph in the hollow of his stomach threatening to poison his entire being—gone! *God made me forget* can be our story too, today.

REDEMPTIVE REMEMBERING

Volf points out that there remained in Joseph, as it does within us today, the need to "remember rightly, [so that] the memory of inhumanities past will shield us against future inhumanities. We must remember wrongdoings in order to be safe in an unsafe world."[6] He calls this redemptive remembering. It is similar to the concept of righteous indignation, for example anger at attacks on God's character or Christ's bride, the church. Volf also points out that Joseph was reminded of the suffering his brothers had caused, yet the divine gift of forgetting his feelings while still remembering the facts of what happened to him enabled him to act with compassion.

The rest of the story, in Volf's words, is Joseph's testimony to the reality of lasting peace:

> Wanting to insure that the precious gift [of sanctified memory] be lost neither on him nor on his posterity, Joseph inscribed it into the name of his son, Manasseh—"one who causes to be forgotten." A paradoxical memorial to forgetting, Manasseh's presence recalled the suffering in order to draw attention to the loss of its memory. It is this strange forgetting, still interspersed with [redemptive] remembering, that made Joseph, the victim, able to embrace his brothers, the perpetrators.[7]

---

6. Volf, *Exclusion and Embrace*, 131.
7. Ibid., 139.

PART I—Winning the Battle

SANCTIFYING SELF AND RENOUNCING SIN

The *second* part of our twofold strategy for winning the battle is to sanctify our inner self—including our memories—and renounce our sinful ways. I am recommending a process of healing prayer and Bible memory work that will enlighten the eyes of your heart, so that you will understand the hope to which the Lord has called you and the riches of his glorious inheritance that he grants among the righteous.[8] Let Scripture be your guide: open the door of your inner self to the empowering strength of the Holy Spirit, open your eyes to the entire breadth and depth of spiritual reality, and open your heart to all the fullness of God.[9] The twenty prayers below provide a helpful beginning for *seeing through the eyes of your heart*. Prayerfully consider each one. Then return to those that you are especially drawn to and pray through them, committing them to memory and submitting wholeheartedly to the direction and transforming power of the Holy Spirit.

Through these prayers the Holy Spirit will be able to search, like a lamp, all the innermost parts of your being and expose secret sin,[10] and unmask any claim to be without sin, so that it can be confessed and forgiven.[11] The Holy Spirit will reveal the sinful themes of your thoughts and the hurtful extremes of your emotions. He will counter the pain of your memories. He will *cover each thought, each emotion and each memory with the power of prayer*. As you pray, you will be removing stones from Satan's fortress (stronghold) if it is present in your inner self. You will be sanctified by the truth—God's word is the truth.[12] May you be wonderfully blessed as the Lord creates in you a pure heart (sanctifies your inner self) and renews a steadfast spirit within you (as you renounce your sinful ways).[13]

8. See Eph 1:18.
9. See Eph 3:16–19.
10. See Prov 20:9 and 27.
11. See 1 John 1:8–10.
12. See John 17:17.
13. See Ps 51:10.

Gracious Father, sanctify my inner self:

"Search me [thoroughly], O God, and know my heart! Try me, and know my thoughts! And see if there is any wicked *or* hurtful way in me, and lead me in the way everlasting."[14]

"Who can understand *his* errors? Cleanse thou me from secret faults."[15]

"Teach me your way, O Lord, and I will walk in your truth; give me an undivided heart, that I may fear your name. I will praise you, O Lord, my God, with all my heart; I will glorify your name forever."[16]

"Show me your ways, O Lord, teach me your paths; guide me in your truth and teach me, for you are God my Savior, and my hope is in you all day long."[17]

"Set a guard over my mouth, O Lord; keep watch over the door of my lips."[18]

May the God of peace sanctify me completely: may my spirit, soul and body be kept blameless, without compromise.[19]

May the peace of the Lord guard my heart and mind in Christ.[20]

Establish my heart blameless in holiness before you.[21]

---

14. Ps 139:23–24, AMP.
15. Ps 19:12, KJV.
16. Ps 86:11–12.
17. Ps 25:4–5.
18. Ps 141:3.
19. 1 Thess 5:23, author's paraphrase.
20. Phil 4:7, author's paraphrase.
21. 1 Thess 3:13, author's paraphrase.

Fill me with the knowledge of your will in all wisdom and spiritual understanding, so that I may walk in a manner worthy of the Lord.[22]

Fill me with all joy and peace as I trust in you, so that I may overflow with hope by the power of the Holy Spirit.[23]

In the name of Jesus, I repent (regret) and renounce (reject) my sinful ways:

- Worship of idols (anything that has become more important to me than fellowship with God)—money, work, relationships, entertainment.
- Rebellion—disrespecting spiritual authority, sowing discord, deceiving others, inflicting harm on any person or group that thwarts my selfish desires.
- Dishonesty—distorting others' actions without regard for the truth, denying biblical warnings about the consequences of my actions, blaming others for my own problems, taking out my frustrations and unresolved anger on others.
- Unforgiveness—of being ignored, belittled, unloved, abandoned.
- Vindictiveness—being judgmental, being quick to take offense, carrying grudges, seeking revenge.
- Untamed tongue—filthy, corrupt, bitter, slanderous expressions and conversations.
- Pride—leaning only on my own understanding, thinking more highly of myself than I should, self-promotion, having an unteachable spirit.
- Worry—fear of the future, disapproval, rejection, losing control.

---

22. Col 1:9–10, author's paraphrase.
23. Rom 15:13, author's paraphrase.

- Besetting sin—abuse (physical, emotional, etc.), jealousy, addiction (alcohol, sexual, etc.), a critical spirit.
- Past or present involvement in occult practices, teaching, rituals, oaths.

We find in the Psalms an authentic account of David's often tortured journey through life, including these self-validated words of wisdom:

> There is nothing in their speech upon which one can rely: their heart is a destructive chasm; their throat is an opened grave; they deceive with their tongue. . . . They have rebelled against Thee.
>
> But let all who take refuge in Thee rejoice. Let them ever shout for joy since Thou dost make a covering over them. Let all who love Thy name be glad in Thee; for Thou, O Lord, dost bless the righteous; with a shield Thou dost surround him with favor.[24]

To suffer through the rebellion of others and be able to take refuge in the Lord and rejoice in Him—that's what we want for ourselves. Be like David.

> And may the Lord of peace Himself
> grant you peace at all times
> under all circumstances.
> The Lord be with you.[25]

---

24. Ps 5:9–12, Berkeley.
25. 2 Thess 3:16, Berkeley.

5

Restoring Peace

How we react in a conflict situation, especially one of prolonged conflict, will have a huge impact on our overall sense of well-being. Should we run away? Should we cave in? Should we fight back? Is it simply a matter of choosing between some form of flight or fight? Or is there another option? What would a good, solid Christian approach look like? Specifically, what biblical models or pathways might we consider for resolving conflict that will significantly enhance our sense of spiritual well-being?

LASTING PEACE

Our goal has to be peace that lasts. The question is, how do we get there? First, we must realize that peace that lasts does not just happen. And it does not stand alone. Long-lasting peace must be pursued, and it always has company. Peace does not just appear out of thin air, and when peace and conflict collide, something beyond human effort must be added to create a truly peaceful, lasting resolution of the conflict.

I submit that righteousness (right standing before God and right living before others) is a necessary precondition for a truly

Restoring Peace

peaceful and lasting resolution. Without it, we have pseudo-peace. We may achieve the absence of conflict while continuing, for example, to practice deceit, dressing people's wounds as though the sin of deceit is not serious and getting along with one another is all that counts. "Peace, peace," we say, when there is no peace as we celebrate our pseudo-reconciliation with others, unashamed of our unaddressed loathsome conduct.[1] The Apostle Peter also has something to say about that:

> Search for peace—harmony, undisturbedness from fears, agitating passions and moral conflicts—and seek it eagerly. —Do not merely desire peaceful relations [with God, with your fellow men, and with yourself].... For the eyes of the Lord are upon the righteous—those who are upright and in right standing with God.[2]

In the context of church conflict, the issue is this: How do we restore peace both in individuals and in the church as a whole? Is our most pressing goal to restore broken relationships of believers, without first restoring individual purity and the purity of the bride? I am opposed to the postmodern idea that reconciliation is the initial goal. I see reconciliation as the ultimate goal. Without restoration from sin, we end up with pseudo-reconciliation. The big question is this: Is this conflict more about broken relationships, or is it more fundamentally about sin?

I strongly agree with G. Campbell Morgan's comment in his book *A First-Century Message to Twentieth Century Christians* that real, long-lasting peace is always based upon purity, that God's order of things is first purity, then peace.[3] I also line up with John White in his book, co-authored with Ken Blue, *Church Discipline That Heals*. They clearly state that restoring sinners takes place when they are restored to righteousness. That is, we are restored

---

1. See Jer 6:13–15; 8:10–12.
2. 1 Pet 3:11–12, AMP.
3. This is a paraphrase of Jas 3:17, taken with modification from G. Campbell Morgan, *First Century Message*, 107.

PART I—Winning the Battle

first to holiness, then to fellowship. True peace is restored through righteousness first, then reconciliation.[4]

What we are looking for is a pathway to (a) restoration of righteousness and reconciliation and (b) potency of influence (power) for long-lasting peace (permanence). We have three models to choose from: Keeping Peace, Making Peace, and Finding Peace. Each model has strong points, some of which overlap and agree with the other models. My intention is to present three different generic forms or types of the peace process, each of which has variations of the predominant themes that are presented. The descriptions that follow, however, are only of the main points—giving the flavor without covering all the possible ingredients of each approach.

THREE MODELS FOR RESTORATION AND RECONCILIATION

Defining Characteristics

- Keeping Peace—Resisting conflict (restraining: controlling, restricting)

- Making Peace—Resolving conflict (repairing: rebuilding, reorganizing)

---

4. White and Blue, *Church Discipline*, 69–70.

- Finding Peace—Redeeming conflict
  (refining: cleansing, purifying)

Comparative Analysis

Keeping Peace

Discord is restrained and corrected, which restores order (righteousness and reconciliation are not addressed).

Making Peace

Broken relationships are reconciled through repentance, which restores fellowship (righteousness is not a primary concern).

Finding Peace

Repentance of sin restores righteousness, which leads to reconciliation.

THREE MODELS FOR POWER AND PERMANENCE

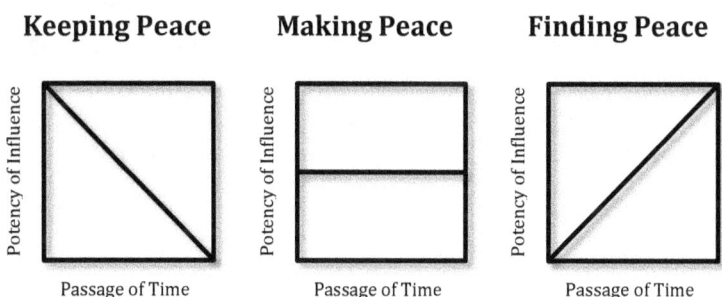

Defining Characteristics

- Keeping Peace—Policing (correcting troublemakers' behavior and restoring order)

PART I—Winning the Battle

- Making Peace—Problem-solving (analyzing systemic problems and prescribing solutions)
- Finding Peace—Praying (sanctifying the inner self and renouncing sinful ways)

Comparative Analysis

Keeping Peace

Most powerful in the beginning of the peace process (through prevention, occupation, and negotiation), but least powerful over time (fundamental causes of the conflict are not dealt with directly).

Making Peace

Starts with less power (through mediation, reeducation, and reconciliation), but maintains its level of power and therefore lasts longer (through human effort for systemic change: reconstructing corporate culture and changing organizational structures).

Finding Peace

Begins with powerlessness but has no limits to its power (through sanctification, restoration, and reconciliation), because prayer connects with the power of the Holy Spirit and increases in power over time (by standing firm in the armor of God against the forces of evil).

I must point out that the idea of keeping peace has often been used as a description of overlooking the upsetting disturbance of peaceful situations. But that is not an effective strategy for restoring peace. It is merely a passive act of convenience, an avoidance or postponement of implementing a proactive model for establishing true peace in such situations. It is nothing more than the creation of pseudo-peace. I am using the Keeping Peace model, however, to describe a strategy for restoring real peace, mostly in combination with other models (e.g., Making Peace and/or Finding Peace) to provide a more lasting peace.

I have also said above that there is overlap and agreement among the models. The most significant example I am aware of is the peacemaking perspective of Ken Sande, in his highly regarded book titled *The Peacemaker: A Biblical Guide to Resolving Personal Conflict*. For example, he presents mediation and arbitration, among other procedures, as alternative ways to resolve disputes—which are Making Peace procedures—and the following biblical principles, which are the basic principles of his approach, and are in almost total agreement[5] with the Finding Peace model:

1. Glorify God (1 Cor 10:31)—"Biblical peacemaking is motivated and guided by a deep desire to bring honor to God by revealing the reconciling love and power of Jesus Christ."
2. Get the log out of your eye (Matt 7:5)—"face up to our own contributions to a conflict before we focus on what others have done."
3. Gently restore (Gal 6:1)—"encourage repentance and restore peace."
4. Go and be reconciled (Matt 5:24)—"Finally, peacemaking involves a commitment to restoring damaged relationships and negotiating just agreements."[6]

Whatever approach we use, we must realize that our strength comes from God, not ourselves. This is strongly conveyed, for example, in the Finding Peace approach. We find peace when we stand firm in the armor of God, when we stand firm in the gospel of peace on the firm foundation of truth and righteousness. We find peace when we stand firm in the face of the onslaught in the midst of the battle, in the presence of the Lord, against the spiritual

---

5. Total agreement depends on changing the final word in the third item, "peace," to "righteousness," which seems reasonable. This keeps the proper sequence in place: repentance, restoration, righteousness, and reconciliation.

6. Taken with modification from Ken Sande, *Peacemaker*, 12–13.

forces of evil. It is a battle on a completely different scale—against a completely different enemy—beyond the earthly context of human conflict and human effort for a peaceful resolution.[7]

The Finding Peace model is a Bible-based, Spirit-formed pathway for following Jesus, both individually and corporately. Consider biblical references to finding peace by reaffirming the future and hope in Jesus;[8] finding Jesus in green pastures and beside still waters, as he guides us in paths of righteousness and through the valley of the shadow of death, so that we will fear no evil for he is with us;[9] and the fact that he himself is our peace, breaking down all barriers and putting to death all hostilities.[10]

All three models have their place and are not mutually exclusive. They can coexist in any combination in the overall process of peaceful resolution of conflict. For example, the Finding Peace model might well be augmented by the emphasis on correction of the Keeping Peace model and the emphasis on systemic analysis of the Making Peace model. And whereas the Finding Peace model is a thoroughgoing, robust biblical perspective—especially when it comes to dealing with the powers of darkness—the Making Peace model can easily incorporate many of the same biblical principles and procedures.

In terms of peace at both the individual and corporate levels, the Finding Peace model is a good example of how the two levels come together:

1. In Christ we have our individual peace.

2. In times of trouble, we find peace not by avoiding trouble or by fighting the troublemakers, but by embracing the Prince of Peace in the midst of the trouble.

3. We restore corporate peace by bringing the peace of Christ into the people's lives who are engaged in the conflict.

---

7. See Eph 6:10–15.
8. See Jer 29:11.
9. See Ps 23:1–4.
10. See Eph 2:14–18.

Restoring Peace

Peace in Christ is a tangible psychological/spiritual condition that marks his followers. As his disciples, we can concretely and confidently bring the peace of Christ into any situation, no matter how troublesome it might be and wherever it might exist. That's what Jesus said—"I have told you all this so that you may find your peace in me. You will find trouble in the world—but never lose heart, I have conquered the world!"[11] And in terms of lasting peace, it is peace in Christ that gives the Finding Peace approach the edge on both power and permanence.

In the final analysis, it all comes down to this: "Cast your burden on the Lord: He will sustain you and never let the righteous be pushed over."[12] The very first words in Psalms fill in some of the details of what "righteous" means in this context:

> Blessed—happy, fortunate and enviable—is the man who walks *and* lives not in the counsel of the ungodly [following their advice, their plans and purposes], nor stands [submissive and inactive] in the path where sinners walk, nor sits down [to relax and rest] where the scornful [and the mockers] gather.[13]

In other words, *walk* and live faithfully in the counsel of the Lord, *stand* firm and actively follow Jesus in the path of righteousness, and *sit down* and find your rest in him—even in the midst of the battle. And you will find peace, your God-given gathering place in green pastures, beside still waters, as he guides you in the path of righteousness and through the valley of the shadow of death.

---

11. John 16:33, Phillips.
12. Ps 55:22, Berkeley.
13. Ps 1:1, AMP.

PART II
Winning the War

6

Toxic Memories

IN THE INTEREST OF *truly lasting peace*, I firmly believe that we must give special attention to putting an end to toxic memories from our painful past. This is a special category—the most relentless, gut-wrenching, debilitating memories from our past. I am defining toxic memories as periodic waves of emotional distress and physical nausea from traumatic circumstances in one's painful past. Over time, a pattern of obsessive, self-imposed, random intrusions of contaminating thoughts and feelings becomes a dreaded reality of existential permanence in everyday life.

Of all the important issues needing closure in the months and years following a season of intense spiritual conflict, unsanctified toxic memories are most likely causing the most ongoing emotional damage. When reconciliation has not yet taken place, and consequences have not happened as God promised they would, it can be very unsettling. That's especially true when forgiveness has not broken the power of the remembered past or produced a sense of physical and emotional integrity. Thus we are left with this most upsetting question: Can I live with my memories of my painful past?

PART II—Winning the War

Some of your painful memories may have already been healed by the prayerful sanctification process. But it's those remaining really bad ones that continue to terrorize you. You hate it when they randomly intrude into your thought life and gnaw at you and numb your emotions and throw you into an emotional tailspin. As long as they continue to poison your thoughts and emotions, you will say, "Peace, peace," when there is no peace! It is imperative that you put an end to your toxic memories.

So far, we have considered what must be done to stop those harmful cultural, social, and family influences, along with personal pathologies and besetting sins that create toxic memories and openings for footholds for demonic deposits in our memory bank. We have already talked about redeeming the conflict that causes the toxic memories; now we are talking about redeeming the memories that result from the conflict—in both cases by bringing them under the lordship of Jesus Christ. Earlier it was in terms of repenting and renouncing our sinful ways; now it is in terms of *reconstructing and reinterpreting* our toxic memories.

I owe a special debt of gratitude to Miroslav Volf, who has done exceptional work in this area. He is well qualified to guide us through these troubled waters. He is a professor of systematic theology at Yale Divinity School and spent eight years in prison in then-communist Yugoslavia, being brutally harassed and interrogated, just because he was a Christian and his wife was an American citizen and therefore, supposedly, a CIA spy.

In his book *The End of Memory*, Volf proposes two categorical questions: *How should we remember?* and *How long should we remember?* I have found these two questions to be the most important questions we can ask.

Memories of wrongs suffered shape our self-perception or identity, but because we can react to them and reconstruct and reinterpret them, we are bigger than our memories. That is important to remember, because we do not want Satan to destroy our personhood through the horror of our memories. God cannot use a moral cipher for his glory!

On the other hand, we can rework our toxic memories for good or for evil—either as a protective shield or a vicious sword. That is also important, especially in *spiritual warfare*. We don't want to let Satan destroy us, but we do not want to allow ourselves to destroy other people either. This is why Volf is adamant about remembering truthfully. So is God, as he speaks to us through the Ninth Commandment: "Thou shalt not bear false witness."[1]

SACRED MEMORIES

A major key to sanctifying toxic memories is filtering them through "sacred memories," or inspirational stories recorded in redemptive biblical history. Volf gives as prime examples the Exodus memory and the Passion (Christ's death and resurrection) memory. By totally immersing ourselves in those sacred memories, we see our own memories through spiritual eyes and see the God of deliverance and the God of salvation, respectively. It transforms us. "Sacred memory shapes identity by drawing [us] existentially into the sacred past.... Sacred memory does not simply bring to mind; it re-actualizes."[2]

The approach I am advocating is based on the replacement theory of substituting an old, negative memory with a new, positive memory. There are essentially two variations on the theme. One focuses on imagining that Jesus was present during the traumatic event and reimagining the event in spiritual terms. The other focuses on reconstructing and reinterpreting the toxic memory of the traumatic events in sacred memory terms. Reliving a traumatic moment in the context of a sacred memory can redirect the state of toxicity into memory reversal of a fearful conditioned response into a faith-filled state of well-being.

Some sacred memories are personal accounts from personal memory. Recall for a moment the Absalom story of betrayal of his father, King David, recounted in chapter 3. What might David's

---

1. Exod 20:16, KJV.
2. Volf, *End of Memory*, 98.

memory have been of that horrible conflict? The answer is found in Psalm 3. The back-story of that psalm was the incredible amount of suffering David endured because of Absalom's sinful years of rebellion, deception, and conspiracy.

It is recorded in Scripture that David *tore his clothes* and *lay on the ground*; he *wept* very bitterly; he *mourned* for his son every day; he *had to flee* to escape from Absalom and the evil he would bring upon David and also Jerusalem; he *went up the Mount of Olives, weeping* as he went, *barefoot and head covered*; he *was told that his counselor was among the conspirators*; he *was pelted and cursed* ("You man of blood, you scoundrel! The Lord has repaid you for all the blood you shed in the household of Saul, in whose place you have reigned. The Lord has handed the kingdom over to your son Absalom. You have come to ruin because [of your own evil]"); he *revealed his distress* ("My son, who is my own flesh, is trying to take my life"); and he *was deeply shaken* by Absalom's violent death ("O my son Absalom! My son, my son Absalom! If only I had died instead of you—O Absalom, my son, my son!").[3]

After all that, David wholeheartedly declared, "You are a shield around me, O Lord; you bestow glory on me and lift up my head. To the Lord I cry aloud, and he answers me from his holy hill. . . . From the Lord comes deliverance."[4] In addition, David testifies that even in the toughest of times he is able to sleep peacefully and awaken with the knowledge that God will sustain him.

Remembering all the personal pain and public humiliation, David chooses to see his situation as God sees it. David manages to do that after experiencing Absalom in person. So can we, when we choose to see through spiritual eyes our experience of Absalom in spirit. Then we must choose, after spiritual conflict with the spirit of Absalom, to immerse ourselves in David's sacred memory of protection and sustainable peace. And we too will find lasting peace.

Caleb is another excellent example of the development of a personal sacred memory.[5] He sets the stage with this recollection:

---

3. See 2 Sam 12:31, 36–37; 15:14, 30–31; 16:6–8, 11–12; 18:33.
4. Ps 3:3–4, 8.
5. See Josh 14:7–14.

"I was forty years old when Moses the servant of the Lord sent me from Kadesh Barnea to explore the land. And I brought him back a report according to my convictions, but my brothers who went up with me made the hearts of the people melt with fear. I, however, followed the Lord my God wholeheartedly."[6] Because of that, Moses swore to Caleb that he would inherit forever the land his feet had walked on. And just as the Lord had promised, he kept Caleb alive for forty-five years while Israel walked in the wilderness.

"So here I am today," Caleb says, "eighty-five years old! I am still as strong today as the day Moses sent me out; I'm just as vigorous to go out to battle now as I was then."[7] He was ready, with the Lord helping him, for battle. Then Joshua blessed Caleb and gave him his inheritance, just as the Lord had promised, because he followed the Lord wholeheartedly. Here are a couple things we can take from Caleb's memory: wholeheartedly follow the Lord, and he will keep his promises; the Lord will keep us strong and help us win the victory.

In the New Testament, Paul gives us a powerful example of seeing through spiritual eyes and reconstructing terror into testimony. He says, "We were so utterly and unbearably weighed down *and* crushed that we despaired even of life [itself]."[8] "But this happened that we might not rely on ourselves but on God, who raises the dead."[9] Paul has steadfast faith that God has delivered them from the most deadly peril, and that he will deliver them from their current situation and in the future. "On him we have set our hope that he will continue to deliver us."[10] From this we can rest assured with joy and confidence: we can rely completely on God; God has rescued us before, and he will do so again, and again. . . .

One of my favorite sacred memories is Joseph's.[11] After many years following his own brothers selling him (at age seventeen)

6. Josh 14:7–8.
7. Josh 14:10b–11.
8. 2 Cor 1:8, AMP.
9. 2 Cor 1:9b.
10. 2 Cor 1:10b.
11. See Gen 37–50.

PART II—Winning the War

into slavery, still remembering how distressed he was pleading for his life, Joseph was now able to weep and sob aloud and tell them not to be distressed themselves with what they had done, "because it was to save lives that God sent me ahead of you."[12] Indeed, God was with Joseph and he had prospered; Pharaoh even put him (at age thirty) in charge of all of Egypt. Seeing his life through God's eyes, Joseph could now unequivocally state that God himself not only *made him forget* his brothers' shameful act, he also *sent him ahead* of them to Egypt to save them from severe famine.

To demonstrate his sincerity, Joseph "threw his arms around his brother Benjamin and wept. . . . And he kissed all his brothers and wept over them."[13] Some time later Joseph reaffirmed that he had forgiven them, saying to them, "You intended to harm me, but God intended it for good to accomplish what is now being done, the saving of many lives. So then, don't be afraid. I will provide for you and your children."[14] And he did (until he died at age 110), living in Egypt along with all his father's family. He meant what he said: "God has made me forget all my troubles and everyone in my father's family"[15]—in other words, all that his brothers had done to him. I'd call that lasting peace!

Here's the thing:

1. God cares about us;
2. Vengeance is not cool;
3. God has our back.

Joseph is an excellent example of taking care to get the facts and the context behind our own memory correct. He did not distort the facts regarding what his brothers did to him, nor did he fabricate new "facts" to make the situation look better in hindsight than it actually was. Volf is right—we must tell the truth! If we don't, we take it out of God's hands and he will not sanctify such

12. Gen 45:5.
13. Gen 45:14–15.
14. Gen 50:20–21.
15. Gen 41:51, NLT.

memories. What we decide is worth remembering must be able to survive scrutiny by the Lord himself.

If we remember truthfully, then we will be able to reconstruct the situation without fear or favor and reinterpret what happened with confidence that God will speak through the facts. That is where sacred memories come in. When we filter our truthfully remembered toxic memories through sacred memories from Scripture, we will be *seeing through God's eyes* as we reconstruct and reinterpret what happened to us (e.g., suffering as Jesus did; entering into his suffering on the cross). And he will give us memories that we can live with! He will make us forget the bad and remember the good.

Sacred biblical memories take hold of our toxic personal memories and wash them clean. The process includes God literally reconstructing these memories. This is how God uses his holy script to completely wash away the stains of the soul-soiling wounds from our remembered past. Possible outcomes of this process can be sorted into the following three categories (with examples):

Purification

- Our deliverance is in God's hands, not ours—we need not rely on evil practices to satisfy our selfish desires.
- Our identity stems from God, so our response to wrongs suffered can be full of grace, not vengeance (see the sacred memory of Joseph).

Protection

- "As God heard the cries of the people of Israel and came to their rescue, so those whose lives have been shaped by the Exodus memory will hear the cries of the afflicted and come to their aid."[16]

16. Volf, *End of Memory*, 108.

PART II—Winning the War

- As the Passion memory reaffirms, no matter how horrendous the wrongs suffered, we can forgive others as we ourselves have been forgiven.

Promise

- "To victims Christ offers his own saving presence. . . . He shields the sufferer's self so that the wrongdoing can neither penetrate to the core of her identity nor determine her possibilities. He promises that her life will acquire wholeness. . . . The memory of the Passion is a memory of returning the wronged to themselves as cherished children of God empowered to emulate God in their own, human way."[17]
- The Lord will shield and sustain us, keep us strong and rescue us (see the sacred memories of David, Caleb and Paul).

Now we turn to our second question: How long should we remember?

FINAL PEACE

Reconciliation. When we can completely let go of memories—both feelings and facts—is inherently tied to the complicated matter of reconciliation. Complete letting go of memories makes sense only after forgiveness has been given and received, sins have been regretted and rejected, justice has been served, and reconciliation has taken place.

Reconciliation makes final peace possible. What kind of peace is another matter. For some it means resolving conflict as quickly as possible, without considering the necessity of repentance of any thing other than petty causes of conflict like taking offense and finding fault. Major sins like rebellion are not even an afterthought. This is a pseudo-peace form of peacekeeping. It certainly is not a thoroughgoing biblical process of peacemaking.

17. Ibid., 118.

I love this advice: "Have salt in yourselves, and be at peace with each other."[18] Those who prefer to take the pseudo-peace approach, however, favor sugar over salt so they can sweeten sour situations and thus momentarily make them palatable. Saltiness, on the other hand, preserves genuine peace. With this approach, we are to be permeated with the purifying, perpetuating influence of holiness. That includes Christian virtue, righteous judgment, and covenantal sacrifice.

Forgiveness starts the whole thing. The complicated matter of reconciliation is fundamentally tied to the complicated matter of forgiveness. It's important to note that forgiveness must be unconditional (i.e., not conditional on the offender's repentance), whereas reconciliation is not. Unconditional forgiveness, however, does not mean tolerating sin (forgiveness is not a substitute for justice) but rather providing a framework for fruitfully pursuing justice. It also means bearing another's sin through intercession. It is more than simply praying, "I forgive him." It is praying, "Father, please forgive him"—in essence asking our Father in heaven to be merciful to him and bless him! Jesus did that on the cross.[19] So did Stephen while his enemies threw stones at him, seconds before he took his last breath.[20]

Forgiveness is fundamentally tied to spiritual well-being. Unforgiveness is a sure sign of deficiency in this area. In fact, being ready to forgive is absolutely essential for spiritual well-being. It is the first of three signs (RAW data, so to speak) that God is at work within you:

- Ready—slow to take offense, quick to forgive
- Able—sanctifying the inner self and toxic memories
- Willing—seeking first the kingdom of God and His righteousness[21]

---

18. Mark 9:50.
19. See Luke 23:34.
20. See Acts 7:60.
21. See Matt 6:33–34.

PART II—Winning the War

Are you ready, able and willing? If so, God is already at work within you. So when the situation presents itself for God-made reconciliation, you have only one decision to make: Join him!

Further complicating the picture, in our postmodern world, "reconciliation" has been made into a divine imperative and surefire solution that applies equally in all cases of conflict. But not all conflicts are the same; all sins are not equal, and justice must be done. Otherwise we end up with pseudo-reconciliation (a false integration or embrace—elbows together but hearts apart).

At a corporate level, have you been in a congregation where everyone is manipulated into confessing sin publicly to prepare the way for forgiveness and group reconciliation? God is not behind manufactured confessions! At an individual level, how often have you "made up"—apologized, been forgiven and promised never to mess up again—only to go through it all over again later? How often have you "reconciled" with hugs and tears only to be burned again when things don't go just right? It might look right, and it might feel right, but is it right only in your own eyes yet not in God's eyes?

I am making a valid distinction here:

- Making short-term peace through man-made reconciliation—the guaranteed "solution" to conflict
- Finding lasting peace in preparation for God-made reconciliation—the ultimate goal—and for final peace (the final stage in resolving a particular conflict)

I am making a further technically valid distinction between lasting peace and final peace. The former refers to conflict management. The latter refers to conflict resolution. We can only take responsibility for what we can control. Leave the rest in God's hands, in his timing. In the absence of genuine terminal reconciliation, we can still forgive those who have sinned against us, sanctify our inner self and toxic memories, forget the feelings but not the facts of our painful past, remember wrongdoings in order to pursue justice and shield against a recurrence, and find lasting peace. All these things can give us peace of mind and settle our emotions, as well as prepare the soil for terminal reconciliation (final peace). In the meantime, "If it is possible, as far as it depends on you, live at peace with everyone."[22] I call this provisional reconciliation: forgiving the people and forgetting the toxic thoughts and feelings—while living at peace with the unresolved contradictory events—from the painful past.

Especially when the wrongdoers stubbornly refuse to repent and reconcile, we must faithfully soldier on with hope for the future. Seeing through spiritual eyes, Miroslav Volf concludes: "Remember wrongs so that you can protect sufferers from further injury, remember them truthfully so as to be able to act justly, and *situate the memories of wrongs suffered into the narrative of God's redemption* so that you can remember in hope rather than despair."[23]

Look at what the Lord has done: "God does not take away our past; God gives it back to us—fragments gathered, stories reconfigured, selves [fully sanctified]."[24] Therefore, *rejoice*, filled with "the goodness of God . . . , and the memories of wrongs will wither away like plants without water."[25]

Rejoice! Turn your eyes upon Jesus:

> Turn your eyes upon Jesus,
> Look full in His wonderful face;
> And the things of earth will grow strangely dim
> In the light of His glory and grace.[26]

---

22. Rom 12:18.
23. Volf, *End of Memory*, 115 (emphasis added).
24. Ibid., 201.
25. Ibid., 214.
26. Lemmel, "Turn Your Eyes upon Jesus."

7
Spiritual Well-Being I

I HAVE DETECTED A pattern in how Satan works. I'm not saying it's the *only way* he works, but it definitely is *a way* that he works. This pattern that I speak of is valid both on the ground and in the heavenlies.

The reality of spiritual conflict/warfare first hit me when our family moved to the state of Washington in the mid-1980s. On the very first day we arrived, we encountered a neighbor with a sociopathic personality similar to but not as extremely dangerous as Mr. Watts, the villainous neighbor in the previously mentioned book *The Devil in Pew Number Seven*. Our neighbor caused that whole first year to be the worst year of our lives: he made verbal threats, cut off our well water, fired off guns at night, and cut down trees on the lot line while we were at church. All those nefarious activities and more—all meant to drive us off our property—made it perfectly clear that Satan did not want us to reclaim the land for Christ. But God had called us there for a purpose, and he prevailed.

Then Satan struck again, roughly twenty years later. In the meantime, we had founded a church (that first met on that same property) that became a strong, faithful, disciple-making small church with a worldwide ministry. How the Lord used his people

Spiritual Well-Being I

to further his kingdom and bring glory to his name is described in detail in our book titled *All Churches Great and Small*. We naturally caught Satan's attention again. My book *When the Bride Is Attacked* (noted earlier) captures the essence of the story of rebellion just as we were retiring, which led to a church split, and how God prevailed once again in spite of demon-influenced conflict. It was, however, a new worst year of our lives.

Putting it all together, I have come to the realization that Satan prefers to attack the strong, not the weak—whether individuals, marriages, or churches. But he attacks the strong through their own or others' weaknesses to undercut their strengths. He attacks individuals and marriages directly through their own weaknesses or indirectly through the weaknesses of others. And he attacks churches directly through their own systemic organizational weaknesses or indirectly through the socio-psychological weaknesses of their members. I can say with assurance that *Satan uses what we give him.*

What I have concluded from this story is this: Satan used the personal pathology of our neighbor to try to demoralize our marriage. And he used the mismanaged personal problems of a few church members to try to destroy our church. But I humbly and with strong conviction submit that in both cases we claimed victory in Christ over Satan's oppression. And Christ protected and preserved our marriage and the faithful remnant of our church—and gave us peace.

Moving forward, I cannot emphasize enough the brute fact that peace does not last unless we deal decisively with those blasted toxic memories that can last a lifetime. Again, I can say with assurance that *God can indeed make us forget.* He can make us forget the toxic thoughts and feelings from our painful past so that we can remember with hope for the future. So we must resist the devil. We must come near to God and he will come near to us, so that the Holy Spirit can purify our heart. And he will lift us up. Praise the Lord! Give him the glory—great things he has done:

PART II—Winning the War

> Great things He hath taught us; great things He hath done,
> And great our rejoicing thro' Jesus, the Son.
> But purer and higher and greater will be
> Our wonder, our transport, when Jesus we see.
>
> Praise the Lord! Praise the Lord! Let the earth hear His voice!
> Praise the Lord! Praise the Lord! Let the people rejoice!
> O come to the Father thro' Jesus, the Son,
> And give Him the glory—great things He hath done![1]

As we reflect back on the great things the Lord has done over the course of our fifty years of marriage, it has been "a long obedience in the same direction," which is the title of a magnificent book written by Eugene Peterson, the translator of the widely acclaimed contemporary version of the New Testament and Psalms titled *The Message*. In his book he cites the one danger that is an ever-present threat to obedience: "the danger that we should reduce Christian existence to ritually obeying a few commandments that are congenial to our temperament and convenient to our standard of living."[2] Our spiritual well-being has been firmly grounded in faithfully seeking to resist both our own ways and the ways of the world—through thick and thin—by drawing close to the Lord so that he can show us the way he works so we can live the way he wants us to live.

Our spiritual well-being has not been about running away, caving in or fighting back. Rather, it has fundamentally been about *following Jesus, standing firm* in the armor of God, and *remaining faithful* to our calling and to the Lord—long obedience in the same direction. Without seeing through spiritual eyes, it would have meant trying to follow Jesus while floundering around in a fog of delusions, diversions, and misdirections. However, by faithfully

---

1. Crosby, "To God Be the Glory."
2. Peterson, *Long Obedience*, 169.

seeing through spiritual eyes, we have been able to see Jesus more clearly and follow him more nearly.

Now we can "look back over heart-breaking trials, scalding tears, mysterious tribulations, with gentle subduedness, without regret, and seeing God in every step of the way."[3] These are the words of Dr. George Watson, author of another marvelous book titled *Soul Food*, published more than one hundred years ago. I am grateful for this powerful little book-for-the-ages for its inspiration and wisdom.

Until now the context of our discussion has been conflict. Now the context is peace. Now is the time to move from finding peace in the midst of and in the memories of traumatic events to embracing well-being in the commonplace events in the ordinary flow of everyday life. We're actually talking about the majority of our lifespan, which occurs *in between* times of severe conflict and momentous calamities. Not trouble free and tension free, but free from having to exert all our time and energy to preserve our physical, psychological, and spiritual well-being.

All three aspects of our humanness overlap and are interconnected. They contribute together to comprise the wholeness of our being. The focus here, however, is on spiritual well-being—the holiness of our being. By that I mean a lifelong process of sanctification: the progressive unfolding and incorporating of our perceptions of the living God into our thoughts and behaviors until our whole being is cleansed and matured into Christlikeness.

Spiritual well-being is seeing through spiritual eyes, which invites the operation of the Holy Spirit upon our perceptions and initiates a spiritual journey of prayer and obedience, simplicity, and humility. It is a journey, not a destination, a pathway for our walk with the Lord. Borrowing from William Faulkner, our spiritual well-being is marked with *footprints*, not achievements. Some footprints are off the path, and some of those become spiritual markers of remembrance of when we turned around and got back on track.

---

3. Watson, *Soul Food*, 13.

PART II—Winning the War

STRAYING OFF COURSE

Certainly spiritual well-being has its ups and downs. But when Christians stray, they need to recognize what path they have strayed from. Peterson likens it to the differences between two types of people on two different pathways: tourists and pilgrims. For *tourists*, being a faithful Christian requires no more than:

- A weekly jaunt to church
- Seeking religious entertainment and diversion through special events like retreats, conferences, and concerts
- Going to see a popular personality or to hear a spectacular new version of truth
- Getting a new experience to somehow expand one's otherwise humdrum life.[4]

For *pilgrims*, being a faithful Christian means walking with the Lord and avoiding all kinds of diversions and misdirections. It is not about programs and personalities—it is about a Person. It requires no less than going to the Source, not to sideshows—it requires "going to God . . . whose path for getting there is the way, Jesus Christ."[5] As it is written: "I am the Road, also the Truth, also the Life. No one gets to the Father apart from me."[6] Pilgrims, when they have strayed, refocus their attention on the Road and ignore the tempting advertisements along the way.

Lukewarmness. In earlier chapters, we saw that in the context of conflict one of the biggest causes of trouble and trauma is rebellion. This is an external, deliberate attack against the path to God. In the context of peace, however, lukewarmness is a really big issue. This is an internal, inexplicable falling away from or avoidance of the path to/of God. It may come as somewhat of a surprise, but while rebellion devours its many, lukewarmness devours its multitudes.

---

4. Peterson, *Long Obedience*, 16.
5. Ibid., 17.
6. John 14:5–6, MSG.

Spiritual Well-Being I

Rebellion is nasty and messy, whereas lukewarmness is unobtrusive and uncomplicated. Though they go about damaging spiritual well-being differently, they have the same results: rebellion causes trauma that impairs spiritual well-being; lukewarmness incubates in the favorable condition of tranquility until it too diminishes spiritual well-being.

> It is not [too] difficult . . . to get a person interested in the message of the gospel; it is terrifically difficult to sustain the interest. Millions of people in our culture make decisions for Christ, but there is a dreadful attrition rate. Many claim to have been born again, but the evidence for mature Christian discipleship is slim. In our kind of culture anything, even news about God, can be sold if it is packaged freshly; but when it loses its novelty, it goes on the garbage heap. There is a great market for religious experience in our world; there is little enthusiasm for the patient acquisition of virtue, little inclination to sign up for a long apprenticeship in what earlier generations of Christians called holiness.[7]

The danger is drifting away as individuals and as a church without even noticing the difference, even though Scripture warns against it: "We must pay more careful attention, therefore, to what we have heard, so that we do not drift away."[8] But make no mistake: the disconnect between lukewarmness and spiritual well-being is huge. It may not seem that way to the casual observer, but the spiritual reality is paralyzing spiritual stagnation. It may still have the appearance of spiritual well-being, but what we actually have is pseudo-spiritual well-being. Scripture spells it out pretty graphically in Jesus' complaint concerning the church at Laodicea:

> I know you inside and out, and find little to my liking. You're not cold, you're not hot—far better to be either cold or hot! You're stale. You're stagnant. You make me want to vomit. You brag, "I'm rich, I've got it made, I

---

7. Peterson, *Long Obedience*, 16.
8. Heb 2:1.

need nothing from anyone," oblivious that in fact you're a pitiful, blind beggar, threadbare and homeless.[9]

Jesus goes on to say: "buy medicine for your eyes from me so you can see, *really* see."[10] Eyes half closed need to become eyes wide open! In other words, see through spiritual eyes your sinful ways. Then, repent: "About face! Run after God!"[11] How could the Laodiceans do that? How can similar churches do that today? Jesus answers the question: "Look at me. I stand at the door. I knock. If you [any person] hear me call and open the door, I'll come right in and sit down to supper with you."[12] Jesus is outside the church looking in. He has been excluded from the operation—the daily life—of his church. And he is asking for just one person to see him and let him in. In essence, they have every thing in the church except Jesus!

Finally, Jesus makes this most gracious and remarkable promise: "Conquerors will sit alongside me at the head table, just as I, having conquered, took the place of honor at the side of my Father."[13] Other translations render it essentially this way: "Overcome as I also overcame, and you will sit down with me on my throne." In other words, overcome the temptations at the center of the curse of lukewarmness, as Jesus also overcame temptation, and take the same pathway that he took to sit down with the Father on his throne. Open your spiritual eyes, open the door for Jesus to enter into the daily living of your life, and open up the pathway to life's *true* riches.

I look at the church at Laodicea and many churches today, and I see:

- Complacency and indifference
- Self-conceit and self-delusion

---

9. Rev 3:15–17, MSG.
10. Rev 3:18.
11. Rev 3:19.
12. Rev 3:20.
13. Rev 3:21.

- Little enthusiasm and urgency
- No passion

I imagine a church—a social club really—situated at the end of a side road off the main road described by Jesus. The people there imagine that they have everything (which attracts tourists to their door), when in fact they have nothing (which keeps pilgrims away from their door). I see Jesus outside the door to that church, knocking. I hear him ask, "Will anyone open the door?" I feel the pain he must feel. And I wonder what I would do if I were inside that church.

First of all, would I open the door? Would you? And if the door were opened, then what? He would enter, and *we* would enter into *his* presence. Enjoying his presence and filled with his Spirit, we would most assuredly be motivated to walk in his way, on his pathway to the Father's throne. All along that pathway, guided by the Holy Spirit, we would see God at work as people from all walks of life accept Jesus as their Lord and Savior and begin to follow him. I can't think of anything more powerful to invigorate our own spiritual life and that of our church. And I think it would be pretty obvious that the rules of that road are just what Jesus has said all along (and we have ignored): "Go and make disciples of all nations, baptizing them in the name of the Father and of the Son and of the Holy Spirit, and teaching them to obey everything I have commanded you."[14]

Jesus made it pretty clear that the marching orders for every Christian and the mission of every church is to make disciples. I am not talking about programs or preaching sermons. I am referring to an intentional, person-to-person process of disciples making disciples who make disciples. This is a major theme of Acts 2. In fact, I see it as the mission of the regular gathering together of Christians at that time. Some would say that the *fellowship* of believers was their mission. I strongly believe, however, that the mission described in Acts 2 is the *followership* of believers. Let's take a closer look.

14. Matt 28:19.

PART II—Winning the War

The curtain rises in Acts 2 on the day of Pentecost and followers of Christ being filled with the Holy Spirit and speaking in foreign languages. Peter boldly takes the opportunity to address the many devout Jews visiting Jerusalem at the time and to urge them to repent and be baptized, receive the Holy Spirit, and become seriously committed followers of Jesus. And three thousand do! And they devote themselves to fellowship and worship with the other believers, praising God and enjoying the favor of the rest of the people in Jerusalem. "And the Lord added to their number daily those who were being saved."[15]

The question is, why did they join the movement? Was it because of *the remarkable fellowship of the community* of believers that was deeply attractive to those outside the community? Or was the Lord daily adding to the community of believers those who were receiving and accepting the witness to *the saving grace of the Lord*?

I believe the community of believers welcomed the people who were responding to Christ as fellow believers, not just as interested seekers. One commentator put it this way: "The single discriminating principle of [the young church's] members was that they all recognized the crucified Jesus of Nazareth as the Messiah. . . . Therefore, we behold the first Christians not only in a state of [outwardly] active fellowship, but also internally changed."[16] The Holy Spirit inclined their hearts to embrace God's gift of regenerating grace, and he transformed their lives!

This is clearly not a picture of church growth based on the attractiveness of the fellowship of the members. Therefore, we should not conclude that fellowship is the primary mission of the successful church—that people will flock to our door because of our *love for one another*. Certainly that is a distinguishing mark of our acceptance of Christ as our Savior and Lord—they will know we are Christians by our love—but the "single discriminating principle" of the biblically successful church is that the members all accept Jesus as their personal Savior and desire to follow him in

---

15. Acts 2:47.
16. Jamieson et al., *Commentary*, 176.

the company of other believers. It is all about their *love of Jesus* and their devoted followership of him as their Lord. Followership precedes fellowship! Followership is the foundation; fellowship is the fruit.

JUNIOR FAITH

Watson uses language in his book that we can use as a framework for disciple-making: the term *junior faith* and the idea that "divine things cannot be had by chance, or under the delusion that God will work them in us anyhow, if we only lie passive in His hand."[17] The former suggests levels of development of spiritual growth; the latter refers to the self-delusion characteristic of lukewarmness. Both are important in the disciple-making process.

Watson's comment concerning delusion fits in well with what Jim Putman and his co-authors write in a training manual titled *Real-Life Discipleship*, from their vantage point of a football game. They put it this way: "Sadly, many Christians believe that the Christian life can be played from the stands. They never get on the field. In other words, they don't have a place of ministry and they don't share Christ with anyone. Instead, they watch their pastors and ministers play, as they are the paid professional players."[18] This is what it looks like: spectators in the stands, players in the game.

It reminds me of Peterson's tourists (spectators) and pilgrims (players). Let's look at this more closely:

1. Tourists (spectators) sit in the pews (the stands/bleachers). They:
    - Show up at church every Sunday (at every game)
    - Sing hymns and choruses (fight songs)
    - Follow the worship leader in singing and responsive readings (the cheerleaders in rousing cheers and chants)

---

17. Watson, *Soul Food*, 65.
18. Putman et al., *Real-Life Discipleship*, 22.

PART II—Winning the War

- Clap their hands in response to a good performance (a great play)
- Stand and raise their hands in praise of their Lord (their athletic heroes)
- Are perked up and prodded along by the worship team (the marching/pep band)
- Celebrate once a year the arrival of their King on a donkey (their homecoming king and queen on a float)
- Listen to the pastor's sermons telling them about the Christian life (the announcer's play-by-play report of the game)

2. Pilgrims (players) are in the game. They:
   - Are not focusing exclusively on being a good person and a positive witness (not just being a good fan and wearing the team logo with pride)
   - Are not passively sitting on the sidelines, unprepared for the harvest (not out of shape, unprepared to play the game)
   - Are intentionally making disciples (actually winning games)

Watson's term "junior faith" also fits in well in the developmental stages of spiritual growth described by Putman et al. Each stage is based on *age resemblance*, not actual age. Spiritual maturity and disciple-making are not correlated with biological age. Consequently, you can make disciples at whatever reasonable age they may be, with a process that is individually tailored to their stage of spiritual growth. And you can even disciple a pre-Christian (a non-Christian, one who is spiritually dead). Putman et al. have made a major contribution by showing that one-on-one disciple-making can be much more effective than assuming that one size fits all, that everyone must proceed at the same pace (like in a class) in their spiritual growth, and that you cannot begin the process before the person to be discipled has accepted the Lord.

Spiritual Well-Being I

There are five stages: Spiritually Dead, Spiritual Infant, Spiritual Child, Spiritual Young Adult, and Spiritual Parent. Two of the stages—Spiritual Infant and Child—look like junior faith to me. First, I am struck by each one's main descriptive characteristic. For the Infant stage it is *ignorance*. For the Child stage it is *self-centeredness*. Second, let's take a look at some representative beliefs and behaviors:

1. Spiritual Infant

    - "Ignorance about what they need and what the Bible says about life and the purpose of a Christian"
    - "Worldly perspective about life with some spiritual truth mixed in"
    - "Belief that they are defined as the culture would define them"

2. Spiritual Child

    - "Belief that people are not caring for them enough"
    - "Belief that feelings are the most important, which leads to spiritual highs and lows"
    - "Confusion and unyielding nature regarding complex issues because they have an incomplete view of biblical subjects"[19]

I believe the church as a whole is filled with Spiritual Infants and Children stuck in biblical ignorance and self-centeredness. They are not moving to the next stages of spiritual maturity. They're stagnant. They're stuck in a religious rut. And many churches seem satisfied with that, as long as the numbers are up and needs are being met.

No program is going to help them. That was dramatically demonstrated fairly recently by an extensive three-year research project at Willow Creek Community Church, a megachurch outside of Chicago.[20] They found beyond any doubt that participation in

---

19. Ibid., 212.
20. Hawkins et al., *Reveal*.

programs created to provide for everyone's needs were not effective in developing the spiritual growth of their members. They had assumed for years that the more involved people are in church programs, the more they become like Christ. They found, however, much to their dismay, that they were *not* making disciples, either in attitude or behavior. In fact, continuing spiritual growth was found to be much more about deepening one's relationship with God and with others through ministry outside the walls of the church. It's significant also that they found the same thing as the research project was expanded to other churches of varying geographic locations, sizes, and ethnic and denominational backgrounds.

This is where focusing on developmental stages of spiritual growth can be much more effective. By meeting Spiritual Infants at their level, Putman et al. point out that we can meet their needs by modeling new habits of a growing believer, teaching about the Christian faith, and giving them personal attention. And by meeting Spiritual Children at their level, we can meet their needs to connect with God, with others, and with their purpose in the church. Then we can focus, as they continue to grow spiritually, on the Spiritual Young Adult and Parent stages, equipping and releasing them for ministry and for intentionally making disciples wherever the Holy Spirit leads them.

Temptation. Let's turn our attention back, briefly, to Jesus' statement to the effect that *overcomers* find victory over the temptations that are at the center of lukewarmness.[21] Overcoming temptation is a major factor contributing to spiritual well-being. We need to understand that spiritual well-being is not a conflict-free zone, and temptation is usually part of the conflict in one way or another. Remember too that Satan usually attacks us at our points of greatest weakness.

It had never occurred to me that experiencing temptation can in and of itself also play a very positive part in developing spiritual well-being—until I discovered Watson's book *Soul Food* and the section titled "Benefits of Temptation." He starts with Scripture: "Count it all joy when ye fall into divers temptations,"[22]

21. See Rev 3:21.
22. Jas 1:2, KJV.

which continues on to say, "knowing *this*, that the trying of your faith worketh patience."²³ Joy and perseverance certainly are significant components of spiritual well-being, but there is more, which Watson spells out in great detail:

> Temptation drives us to a deep, serious study of ourselves; it makes us take ourselves all to pieces, to analyze our affections, our wills, our motives, our propensities; it makes us search the quality of our actions, thoughts, words; it makes us scrutinize our real chance for heaven or hell; it makes us dig in solitude to the very secret foundation of our character.
>
> Temptation compels us to study the awful nature of sin; it makes us trace the danger of wrong affections, of evil thoughts, of improper words; it opens our eyes to see the hell-fire that stealthily sleeps in so-called little sins. To be thoroughly tempted is the pathway to a thorough knowledge of ourselves and of the malignity of sin.²⁴

In other words, being tempted in and of itself is not straying off course, a trial that is off the pathway of God. It is in fact an important part of spiritual well-being. Watson goes on to say:

> Temptation . . . withers our cleverness, cauterizes our smartness, teaches us true [humility]. . . . But for the severe temptations, the soul would go skipping along, gloating over its own pretty piety, full of self-admiration. As a severe case of small-pox will prevent a pretty face from standing before a mirror, so terrible temptations prevent holy souls from admiring their own graces.²⁵

Watson caps it off with this magnificent statement of faith and hope: "It is God's design that we shall have the most perfect victory on the very points where we have been the weakest."²⁶ What an extraordinary thought that is to hold on to! What a powerful reminder that although Satan will tempt us, we can use his attack on the very points where we are weakest to gain the victory.

23. Jas 1:3, KJV.
24. Watson, *Soul Food*, 68.
25. Ibid., 68–69.
26. Ibid., 67.

8

Spiritual Well-Being II

FOR THE CHRISTIAN, SPIRITUAL well-being highlights the holiness of one's being, or Spirit-formed well-being. It refers to the guidance of the Holy Spirit in the lifelong process of maturing in Christlikeness. It is the Holy Spirit-formed well-being of staying on the path of one's faithful walk with the Lord. And finally, it moves one toward final peace in the form of *reconciliation*, the final stage of a conflict resolution process, as well as ultimate well-being in the form of *rest*—a place of grace here and glory hereafter.

It is reasonable to conclude from a biblical perspective that Spirit-formed well-being is a spiritual journey—regardless of the presence or absence of conflict—of arriving at and entering into God's rest. This is the very essence of truly Spirit-formed well-being: believing faith and holy living, inward peace and joy, and freedom from all fears and sorrows.[1] Jesus made all of this possible for us. He died for us, and he lives for us today:

> Come to me. Get away with me and you'll recover your life. I'll show you how to take a real rest. Walk with me and work with me—watch how I do it. Learn the unforced rhythms of grace. I won't lay anything heavy or

---

1. See Heb 4:1–11.

Spiritual Well-Being II

ill-fitting on you. Keep company with me and you'll learn to live freely and lightly.[2]

There is a fundamental choice to be made. And this is it—a choice between the physical realm and the spiritual realm: "So we fix our eyes not on what is seen, but on what is unseen. For what is seen is temporary, but what is unseen is eternal."[3]

For example, don't be deterred or seduced by things seen that seem either wrongheaded or wonderful by the world's standards—they are culture-bound and subject to change. Rather, our lives need to be determined by things unseen, of everlasting value. Another example is when things seen seem irreversibly tragic and the choice is between dead-end physical reality (as seen through man's eyes) and death-defying spiritual reality (as seen through God's eyes): trauma or triumph from the past; discouragement or encouragement in the present; pessimism or optimism about the future.

The choice, in the final analysis, is between life and death: "I have set before you life and death, blessings and curses. Now choose life, so that you . . . may love the Lord your God, listen to his voice, and hold fast to him."[4] Now, choose life! Jesus is the Way, the Truth, and the Life. He is our life! Therefore I say again, "Turn your eyes upon Jesus."

STAYING ON COURSE

To get a better handle on Spirit-formed well-being and to tie things together a bit, I would like to roll up Peterson's descriptions of joy, perseverance, and obedience into a composite word-picture:

- It is "not a spurt of good feelings that comes when the weather and the stock market are both right on the same day."

---

2. Matt 11:28–30, MSG.
3. 2 Cor 4:18.
4. Deut 30:19–20.

PART II—Winning the War

- It is the steadfast joy "that comes from feeling good not about yourself but about God."
- It is the result of "making a map of the faithfulness of God, not charting the rise and fall of our enthusiasms."
- It is the fruit of faithful obedience, "not a stodgy plodding in the ruts of religion, [but] a hopeful race toward God's promises."[5]

In short, Spirit-formed well-being is at its core a Holy Spirit-guided journey of faith along the pathway that God has provided for a long obedience in the same direction, delighting in seeing God at work and being involved in what he is doing. We can complement this definition with the four components mentioned earlier: prayer, obedience, simplicity, and humility. Let's see what George Watson has to say about them, along with some insights from Eugene Peterson one hundred years later.

FOUR CORE COMPONENTS

Prayer and obedience. As we journey along God's pathway, prayer and obedience are fundamental for staying on course: pray and obey. Earlier, I quoted Watson's strikingly detailed description of the experience of being tempted and his conclusion that it can be included as an important part of well-being. Now he opens our spiritual eyes to the full, unedited reality of being in *prayer*:

> Sometimes I begin praying with a weary, dull feeling; my thoughts seem dry, my affections seem becalmed, and this dryness lingers for ten or twenty minutes, but by fixing my thoughts on God and asking Him to breathe in me the very prayer which will most please the Father, and then by patiently waiting and pleading the infinite merit of [Jesus], by and by the brightness begins to come; the heart is melted, tears of love and thanksgiving flow; an inexpressible sweetness settles into *all my being.*

5. Peterson, *Long Obedience*, 97, 101, 133, 168.

> Then all difficulties, all sorrows, all hardships, all burdens, all loneliness, all anxiety of every sort and degree, sink away below the horizon, and I find myself in a vast prairie of blooming flowers, and magnificent vistas, and clear skies, and singing birds, and gently flowing streams, and *my whole being* seems dissolved into great drops of love.[6]

I really like Watson's sense of the "whole-being" aspect of Spirit-formed well-being. I also appreciate Peterson's expansion of the phrase "patiently waiting" in Watson's description of being in prayer. Peterson begins by quoting Scripture: "I pray to GOD—my life a prayer—and wait for what He'll say and do. My life's on the line before God, my Lord, waiting and watching till morning, waiting and watching till morning."[7] Then he goes to say that "there is more than a description of reality here, there is a procedure for participating in it. The program is given in two words: *wait* and *watch*. . . . *Wait* and *watch* add up to *hope*."[8]

When we can say with the psalmist, "my life [is] a prayer," it implies that we are prayerfully *being* aware of blessings and alert to dangers, as well as prayerfully waiting and watching for what God is *doing*. That is *hope*. It is real, not delusional, confident expectation that the Holy Spirit will guide our prayers and that God will keep his promises. He will never forsake us.

When the Holy Spirit inhabits our prayer life, he is activating our spiritual eyesight. This brings both our imaging of the present and our imagining of the future under the lordship of Jesus Christ. We can call this *sanctified imagination*. When we take every thought captive to the Word of God and pray Scripture (e.g., pray sacred memories as our own), we move from framing in our mind our own pictures of reality to framing pictures of the kingdom of God. We begin to see spiritual reality with our spiritual eyes wide open.[9]

---

6. Watson, *Soul Food*, 121–22 (emphasis added).
7. Ps 130:5–6, MSG.
8. Peterson, *Long Obedience*, 142.
9. See Allen, *Gazing into Glory*.

PART II—Winning the War

When we frame our mental pictures with unsanctified imagination, we will inevitably get into trouble with *obedience*. If, however, one were to frame one's mental picture of obedience with sanctified imagination, it might look very much like Watson's portrayal of fishers of men recorded in Luke 5. One day, while Jesus is teaching by the Lake of Gennesaret, he notices two fishing boats at the water's edge. So he gets into one of the boats, belonging to Simon, and asks him to launch out from the shore. *Launch*, Watson suggests, would be like moving out under the guidance of the Holy Spirit. *From the shore* implies leaving behind other concerns and desires.

Then Jesus tells Simon to put out into deep water and let down their nets. *Into deep water* does not indicate how deep, however. "The depth into which we launch will depend upon how perfectly we have given up the shore and the greatness of our need, and the apprehension of our possibilities. The fish were to be found in the deep, not in the shallow water. So with us; our needs are to be met in the deep things of God."[10] *Down their nets*, then, "signifies letting down our gifts, talents, occupations, into the will of God . . . beyond our vision, trusting all results with Him."[11]

Simon answers that they had fished all night and caught nothing. Nevertheless, at Jesus' word he lets down the nets. *All night, and nothing* creates the expectation that God will take failure, loss, or disappointment and turn it into success. *At Jesus' word* embodies Simon's act of obedience: "Right on the spot of past defeat, over the same waters, with the same net, in the same boat, without any visible signs of success, we are to drop ourselves into His will. Simply obey, and leave it with Him."[12] And they caught so many fish that their nets began to break, and they filled both boats so full that they began to sink!

If we intend to frame in our mind other pictures from Scripture of the kingdom of God, in addition to this one from Luke 5,

10. Watson, *Soul Food*, 86.
11. Ibid., 87–88.
12. Ibid., 88–89.

we will do well to heed Peterson's guidelines for reading Scripture. They included reading imaginatively, prayerfully, and obediently.

We must read Scripture *imaginatively*, bringing our personal experiences into the story so we can observe what happens to us in this biblical context. But we must be careful not to reconfigure the biblical story into our own story, but rather to let the biblical story reconstruct our story. "Imagination is the capacity we have of crossing boundaries of space and time, with all our senses intact, and entering into other God-revealed conversations and actions, finding ourselves at home in Bible country."[13]

We must read Scripture *prayerfully*, not just to gather information, but for our personal formation. "The Bible is not so much God telling us some *thing*—some idea, some fact, some rule—as God speaking life into us. Are we listening? Are we answering? Bible reading is prayed reading."[14]

Finally, we must read Scripture *obediently*.

> Well-meaning people have told us that the Bible is useful, and so we pick it up. We adapt, edit, sift, summarize. We then use whatever seems useful and apply it in our circumstances however we see fit. We take charge of the Bible, using it as a toolbox to repair our lives or as a guidebook for getting what we want or as an inspirational tract to enliven a dull day.
>
> But . . . the Author of the book is writing *us* into *his* book, we aren't writing *him* into *ours*. . . . This is an immense world of God's salvation that we are entering; we don't know enough to "apply" anything. Our task is to obey, believingly, trustingly obey. Simply obey.[15]

Simplicity and humility. We cannot use the Bible as a toolbox or as a guidebook, on our own terms, for what suits us best. We need to simply obey. In fact, we need simplicity in most areas of our lives. That includes the area of Spirit-formed well-being, which would be greatly enhanced if we could uncomplicate life by

---

13. Peterson, *Long Obedience*, 205.
14. Ibid.
15. Ibid., 205–6.

concentrating more on being than on doing. If we could somehow learn to just let go and let God work in us, and through us, and for us according to his will for our lives. Like Watson says:

> We have to learn over and over again to cease from all our planning, all our imaginings of ways and means, all our uneasiness or care, and just calmly, sweetly, patiently, humbly "let God" manage and work in us and for us along lines beyond all our dreaming. . . . We have to learn to "let God" do in us and for us, over a great many times and in a variety of things . . . [so that] we can be ready at every sharp turn and under all sorts of circumstances to "let God" mould and move all our welfare according to His best purpose.[16]

In short, Spirit-formed well-being means letting God. And, it means being grateful for the gifts he gives us so we can give to others and give back to him. "God's best gifts are the simplest, such as air and light and water and bread. So, in religion, the greatest things are unmixed love, pure humility, fixed obedience, a single eye to please God."[17] This is what the kingdom of God is like. It's where quality trumps quantity, and where little trumps big. Watson makes the point that God proves his divinity by the priority he gives to small, simple things.

Watson writes that immensity and splendor hide God, smothering him with all the magnitude and glitter. The created is given more glory than the Creator, and the Holy Spirit "finds Himself slighted, and quietly hunts up little people and little opportunities, where God alone can get the glory. In every age of the world, the Holy Spirit has been traveling away from big things into the small, in order to find places where God alone shall be exalted."[18]

Isn't that especially true with small churches? Watson refers to them as "little works wrought in obscurity," where self-glorifying distractions are more easily weeded out. He portrays a beautiful picture of "a walled-in garden to sow down with deeds and words

16. Watson, *Soul Food*, 104–5.
17. Ibid., 53.
18. Ibid., 51.

and manners and looks, out of a loving, tender spirit, with no incentive but love, and no purpose but to please Him."[19]

As individuals, how can we best live our lives with no incentive but love and no purpose but to please the Lord? Watson's answer is this: "It is the unpremeditated and instinctive actions and words that reveal the reality of what is in us, and not those large, conspicuous things for which we especially arm ourselves. The most essential grace for a human being is *humility*."[20]

I used to think this or that person would make a great Christian because he or she was so sociable, likeable, energetic, etc.—a great personality that God could use for the cause of Christ. Now, of course, I realize that it's not about the personality characteristics of people who may or may not fit God's fancy. He wants the person, not the personality. He will fit his own characteristics into the person's own individual form of personhood, but he and he alone will decide what will and will not need to be changed.

Peterson points out that some *pruning* will always be needed. "It gets rid of that which looks good to those who don't know any better, and reduces the distance between our hearts and their roots in God."[21] The pruning will undoubtedly take place in our unsanctified self through the process of repenting and renouncing our sinful ways. It will also involve seeing properly, through spiritual eyes, when we (in Peterson's words) have removed God from the picture and replaced him with our own crudely sketched self-portrait. And it will substitute any trace of pseudo-humility with the real thing.

Watson gives us a graphic picture of how God will accomplish this transformation. "God locks us in alone with Himself" in a furnace "and thereby saturates us with the Holy Spirit."[22] With the Holy Spirit's guidance, we are brought face to face with the sinful ways in our unsanctified self that he exposes for us to die to. He exposes only those things that will most perfectly transform

19. Ibid., 52.
20. Ibid., 49.
21. Peterson, *Long Obedience*, 149.
22. Watson, *Soul Food*, 82.

Part II—Winning the War

us into Christlikeness. But while he will not allow us to choose for ourselves what would undoubtedly be most comfortable and safe to throw into the fire, he will not allow the fire to consume us. He only does what is best for us. He "fits the furnace to our frame."[23]

God fits the pruning to our form. He fits the furnace to our frame.

> Instead of fretting over our peculiar make-up, or criticising that of others, let us remember that God will not undo the mechanism or form of our individualism, but His plan is to purge away all sin. . . . [Do not] chafe or wrestle with your formation, but . . . always yield it to the possession of the Holy Spirit. [That] is the way to victory and blessing.[24]

That is the way to Spirit-formed well-being. As you continue your spiritual journey, keep your feet on the ground and your eyes on the road. That's humility, and that's obedience. They are a solid start for Spirit-formed well-being, and for entering into God's rest.

> I serve a risen Savior, He's in the world today;
> I know that He is living, whatever men may say.
> I see His hand of mercy, I hear His voice of cheer,
> And just the time I need Him, He's always near.
>
> He lives, He lives! Christ Jesus lives today!
> He walks with me and talks with me along
>   life's narrow way.
> He lives, He lives, salvation to impart!
> You ask me how I know He lives?
> He lives within my heart![25]

---

23. Ibid., 81.
24. Ibid., 131.
25. Ackley, "He Lives."

9

Meaningful Memories I

MEMORIES ARE WOVEN INTO the fabric of the biblical record, both the Old and the New Testaments. Two major memorable events stand out as central in redemptive biblical history: Israel's exodus from Egypt and Jesus' death and resurrection. The history of Israel hinges on the covenantal memory—an appointed feast for all time—of the exodus,[1] and the history of Christianity hinges on the memory of the cross. For Christians Jesus' words, "This [bread] is my body given for you; do this in remembrance of me,"[2] plus "This cup is the new covenant in my blood; do this, whenever you drink it, in remembrance of me,"[3] are at the core of the sacrament of Communion.

Two kinds of memories are at the core of spiritual well-being: redemptive memories (see chapter 4) and meaningful memories. Meaningful memories are directly related to time and how we live in the present. For instance, how we remember the past can bless us or dishearten us in the present. We can, of course, keep that

---

1. See Exod 12:14.
2. Luke 22:19b.
3. 1 Cor 11:25b.

PART II—Winning the War

on the positive side by reinterpreting and reconstructing the past within biblical guidelines and with the guidance of the Holy Spirit.

Similarly, when we mold and shape our lives in the present in accordance with God's promises, we create meaningful memories for the future. This is seeing through the cloud of crisis and uncertainty of living in today's complex and confusing world, and picturing in our mind's eye the peace and hope for the future that is God's revealed desire for us as believers. Ponder these thoughts and their possibilities:

> Trust in the Lord and do good.
> Then you will live safely in the land and prosper.
> Take delight in the Lord,
> and he will give you your heart's desires.
> Commit everything you do to the Lord.
> Trust him, and he will help you.[4]

> The Lord directs the steps of the godly.
> He delights in every detail of their lives.
> Though they stumble, they will never fall,
> for the Lord holds them by the hand.[5]

> Put your hope in the Lord.
> Travel steadily along his path.[6]

I want to make a clear distinction here. This is not prooftexting the details of our personally preferred future but, rather, revelation-testing all our options. That means that the better we understand God's promises and practice their conditions in our daily lives, the more meaningful our memories will be.

To see the total picture, we need to understand not only God's promises but also his creation. To do this it is helpful to adopt the view that all truth is God's truth. That means we must look through our spiritual eyes at scientific studies as well as biblical studies to

---

4. Ps 37:3–5, NLT.
5. Ps 37:23–24.
6. Ps 37:34.

fill in some of the blanks that our study of Scripture cannot provide. What I am saying, without hesitation, is that science can help us find meaning in spiritual matters.

My integrative perspective is enthusiastically shared by Malcolm Jeeves, a renowned expert in neuropsychology, in his most recent book, *Minds, Brains, Souls and Gods*:

> If we remember that the God we worship is, as we are taught in Scripture, the Creator and Sustainer of all that is, then the knowledge that our God chooses to give us through Scripture cannot ultimately conflict with the knowledge he chooses to give us by using the minds he has given us to understand his universe. Since we believe that God is the author of all truth, the accounts from the two sources will ultimately not conflict, though there will be many puzzles and much hard thinking along the way.[7]

The brain is the new frontier in science, and one of the most radical developments is the new science of how the mind makes meaning. Revolutionary research is being conducted on what is called embodied simulation and, of particular interest to me, finding meaning through metaphors. This is all detailed beautifully by Benjamin Bergen in his book *Louder Than Words*. Although Bergen does not view his research through spiritual eyes, I am finding that his work is very helpful in understanding spiritual metaphors and how God reveals his truths through them. This new research is something I would have greatly appreciated years ago, when I was formulating my own model for integrating science and Christian faith (psychology and theology), which I referred to as *embodied integration*.[8] Embodied in that case meant lived out/experiential, not just abstract/conceptual. With that in mind, I will construct in this chapter and the next an embodied integration of the scientific concept of simulation and the theological concept of sanctification as a guide for creating meaningful memories that will undergird our spiritual well-being for years to come.

---

7. Jeeves, *Minds, Brains, Souls*, 192.
8. See Farnsworth, *Integrating Psychology* and *Wholehearted Integration*.

PART II—Winning the War

EMBODIED SIMULATION

Bergen's use of the word *embodied* says that the way our mind works and the way we understand meaning are both inextricably tied to our bodies. All aspects of finding meaning are manifested in identifiable areas of the brain. This is big news! *Simulation* refers to creating internal mental experiences that use the same areas of the brain that are used during interaction with external realities.

Bergen presents a plethora of significant research findings, among which I find the following helpful in my pursuit of valid spiritual realities and relevant meaning in spiritual matters:

1. Internal mental experiences do in fact use the same parts of the brain that are dedicated to directly interacting with motor, visual, and auditory external realities.

2. Mental experiences of both seeing and performing actions are created without actually being on site and without actually moving.

3. Repetitions create echoes for reusing brain patterns produced during previous interactions with external realities, substantially reinforcing their reoccurrence in the future.

4. When dealing with language, "meaning . . . isn't just abstract mental symbols; it's a creative process, in which people construct virtual experiences—embodied simulations—in their mind's eye."[9]

5. Imagination and memory also involve embodied simulation:

   > Visualizing an action reuses parts of the brain that actually control those imagined actions. And this is a pervasive property of the mind. We also use our brain's action and perception systems for memory; when we recall events, we reconstruct what they felt like, looked like, or sounded like, and this again uses parts of the brain whose primary duty is to allow us to perceive or participate in events of these types in the first place.[10]

9. Bergen, *Louder Than Words*, 16.
10. Ibid., 25–26.

6. To understand metaphors, we "construct embodied simulations that are slightly less detailed than ones we construct for literal language but that are no less motor or perceptual."[11]

Bergen says right after this last quote, "There's something very exciting about this finding." I agree, for the simple fact that the Bible contains so many metaphors that must be unpacked to benefit from the spiritual truths that they contain. Metaphors can be defined as implied comparisons that liken one thing to another; illustrations of material realities that express spiritual truths and reveal spiritual realities.

Here's a sampling of what they look like in the Bible:

- "A mighty fortress is our God."[12]
- "You are my hiding place and my shield."[13]
- "Put on the full armor of God."[14]
- "They will soar on wings like eagles."[15]
- "I will make you fishers of men."[16]
- "The Lord is my shepherd [to feed, guide, and shield me]; I shall not lack.

  He makes me lie down in (fresh, tender) green pastures; He leads me beside the still *and* restful waters.

  He refreshes *and* restores my life—my self; He leads me in the paths of righteousness [uprightness and right standing with Him—not for my earning it, but] for His name's sake.

  Yes, though I walk through the [deep, sunless] valley of the shadow of death, I will fear *or* dread no evil; for You are with

---

11. Ibid., 208.
12. Ps 46:7, as expressed in a hymn.
13. Ps 119:114, AMP.
14. Eph 6:11.
15. Isa 40:31.
16. Matt 4:19.

me; Your rod [to protect] and Your staff [to guide], they comfort me.

You prepare a table before me in the presence of my enemies; You anoint my head with oil [as the Lord would anoint His 'sheep' with the Holy Spirit Whom oil symbolizes, to fit them to engage more freely in His service and run in the way He directs, in heavenly fellowship with Him]; my [brimming] cup runs over.

Surely *or* only goodness, mercy *and* unfailing love shall follow me all the days of my life; and through the length of days the house of the Lord [and His presence] shall be my dwelling place."[17]

The Amplified Version of the twenty-third Psalm does give us some help in appreciating the incredible depth and beauty of God's Word. And metaphors are a great way to convey that. What is exciting to me is the now-established fact that the meaning of the language of the Bible includes and is more than what is contained in abstract symbols. Finding meaning is not just a word association process. It is a creative mental process that involves our physical brain's action and perceptual systems. It means that even imagination and memory involve embodied simulation. No longer can it be said, "That's just your imagination," like it's just a stab in the dark! To imagine can mean to invent or make up, but it also means to grasp reality! Imagining uses the same parts of our brain that we use to directly interact with motor, visual, and auditory external realities.

Metaphors play an important role in intentionally creating meaningful memories. Metaphors enhance and enrich the meaning of memories and in the process engage our brain's action and perception systems to reconstruct what something felt like, looked like, and sounded like. This finding among the six listed above has the most direct relevance in terms of spiritual well-being. It substantiates the role of Bible memory work in creating

---

17. Ps 23, AMP.

redemptive memories. It supports the use of sacred memories in blotting out toxic memories, in converting debilitating nightmares into *spiritual markers* or powerful testimonies of God's presence. And it verifies and exemplifies our God-given ability to make and rehearse meaningful memories or spiritual markers in all of life's circumstances.

INTEGRATING SCIENCE AND FAITH

Bergen refers to seeing through our mind's eye. What I am interested in is seeing through our *spiritual* mind's eye. I am making a crucial point here, one that Bergen refuses to recognize. I am referring to his comments under the heading "How We Got to Be This Way." His underlying answer is evolution, along with a put-down of what he calls the "God myth." To this I say, "Au contraire!" God created our brains and what they do. There is absolutely no reason to kick God out of his creation.

What Bergen seems to be saying is that meaning is encoded in our body language, and we should listen to what our body is telling us. I see no reason that the Holy Spirit cannot be involved in such a process—i.e., we can sense his presence with all of our senses. When we acknowledge that God is at the very center of the embodied simulation process, it opens a lot of doors. For example, studying the Bible, praying, worshiping, giving, serving, forgiving, making disciples—all benefit from the echoes created by repetitions of using brain patterns produced during previous interactions with external realities, greatly reinforcing their reoccurrence in the future. The Holy Spirit has lots to work with—all those sights, sounds, thoughts, and feelings. Christian living involves much more than having righteous thoughts.

Satan, of course, also has lots to work with. Evil thoughts are created by embodied simulation too, not just good ones. We can see, however, that the Holy Spirit also has solid ground on which to operate in exposing demonic spiritual realities, by opening our imaginations to the very real possibilities of spiritual conflict. And he gives us the spiritual weapons to fight the real enemy. This should give us even greater confidence that we can win the battle, and that we can win the war.

We can also win the peace. This relates directly to dealing with toxic memories. The reason these memories are so horrific, so upsetting, so poisonous, and so unrelenting is precisely the fact that they are lodged in the very real brain patterns that were used in responding to the original physical and emotional trauma. Again, the Holy Spirit gives us all we need to find real, lasting peace.

A new book by Ken and Jeanne Harrington, titled *Deliverance from Toxic Memories*, presents detailed research on chemical changes and electrical impulses in the brain, caused by a variety of stressors, and treatment for their relief. The scientific findings support a scientific-spiritual perspective on the development and treatment of toxic memories. The authors place their analysis within the framework of our five physical senses and three *spiritual senses*. In the latter they include conscience (judging right from wrong), communion (connecting with God), and intuition (discovering truth without reasoning, and receiving inspiration from God).[18]

I would construct this somewhat differently. I am particularly interested in the idea of spiritual senses, but I would frame them within the process of Spirit formation in connecting with God: all spiritual senses are vehicles for God-given inspiration through communion with the Holy Spirit. I would propose these four spiritual senses:

- Conscience—judging right from wrong
- Intuition—preconscious tending toward relationship with someone or something
- Imagination—finding meaning
- Reason—discovering truth

I have retained two of the Harringtons' three proposed spiritual senses. However, I have changed the definition of intuition to better fit the inclusion of imagination and reason in my list of

---

18. Harrington and Harrington, *Deliverance from Toxic Memories*, 35–44.

spiritual senses. I will develop the functions and interaction of imagination and reason in chapter 10.

The Harringtons, in the meantime, only confuse the issue: "Reasoning involves thinking, which is a soulish activity; perceiving involves discerning, which is a spiritual activity."[19] The way I see it, all four spiritual senses are governed by brain *and* Spirit activity. Reasoning and perceiving—as well as conscience, intuition, and imagination—are *all* both physical and spiritual activities. And they are also subject to both demonic influence and Spirit formation—working against each other. That's how we get spiritual warfare.

How might these spiritual senses be affected by the evil end of the spiritual spectrum? Remember, Satan can counterfeit all of these spiritual senses. Also, remember that Satan is the author of confusion. How, then, does he deceive and confuse us? I stand by my earlier statements in this book: Satan uses what we give him—our weaknesses and mismanaged personal problems—and he targets those specific areas within our unsanctified self and converts them into strongholds to use for his own diabolical purposes. God-inspired imagination and reason are two of our greatest weapons against him!

---

19. Ibid., 40.

10

Meaningful Memories II

IMAGINATION IS A LINK between two realms of reality: the natural realm and the spiritual realm. We love to imagine things. A new house. A better job. Relief from pain. Peaceful relationships. Vacationing in Hawaii. Winning the big game. The list goes on. Similarly, we might imagine these sorts of things: God's provision, a new or renewed sense of calling, healing of toxic memories, lasting peace, rest in the Lord, and victory in Christ. All of these things are important and very real to us. And sometimes they actually happen, bringing both realms into play at the same time. We get what we wish/pray for.

Imagining in both the natural and the spiritual realms involves the same brain/mental capacities, whether the images are concrete or abstract, natural or spiritual. In other words, all imagery—visual (sights), auditory (sounds), and motor (movements)—operates under the same rules. This does not mean, however, that imagery in either realm is necessarily true or from God.

Daydreaming is an excellent example of imagery interfering with and/or misrepresenting present reality. Many of us have been there/done that—"zoning out" during sermons or fantasizing about a bad situation being better than it is, for example.

Visualization, on the other hand, is a good example of empowering the hoped-for realization of a future reality. This is a powerful technique in sports: programming the brain to do the same thing it has done over and over in actual practice (sinking the free throw, making the putt, winning the race, etc.).

What exactly is imagination? How does it enter into our knowledge of God and our growth as Christians? Let me ask a more personal question: Have you had difficulty with a troublesome passage in Scripture and after a good deal of thought still not been able to grasp its meaning, and you even doubted the possibility of ever getting it right? Could it be that you had difficulty finding the meaning of the passage because you couldn't imagine it? Consider that when the door is closed, the key to opening the door is allowing the Holy Spirit—through your imagination—to lead you to the meaning of the passage, and to deeper knowledge of God and growth in your Christian life.

The issue is, couldn't you just reason your way to the meaning of the passage? I'll let acclaimed Christian author C. S. Lewis's paradigm-shifting insight answer that: "For me, reason is the natural organ of truth, but imagination is the organ of meaning. *Imagination . . . is not the cause of truth, but its condition.*"[1] The word *organ* is similar to the spiritual senses discussed in chapter 9 and is used here as a means for performing a specific function or action; in this case imagination is for finding meaning and reason for discovering truth. I believe this brilliant insight is of the utmost importance.

Michael Ward, in a recent *Christianity Today* article, put it this way: "For Lewis, this is what the imagination is about: . . . the ability to identify meaning, to know when we have come upon something truly meaningful."[2] In other words, we need imagination to separate the meaningful from the meaningless, to make sense out of nonsense. That's where reason comes in, where we judge whether something is actually true or false (not just truly meaningful). However, the imagination-to-meaning-to-reason-

---

1. Lewis, "Bluspels and Flalansferes," 265 (emphasis added).
2. Ward, *Lewis*, 38.

to-truth formulation must have something else added to more fully apprehend truth: supernatural revelation—the inspiration of the Holy Spirit throughout the entire process.

In short, we must acknowledge the possibility of something before we can imagine it and embrace its meaning, before we can reason about it and accept it as true. And when God is involved throughout the process, we can state with confidence that "truth . . . is both imaginative and rational. That which God has joined, let no man put asunder."[3]

Compared with the straightforward relationship between imagination and reason, the relationship between imagination and meaning is rather complex. That would be because of *context*. David Kelsey in his book *Imagining Redemption* sees three different contextual realities that affect meaningful imagination: concrete situation, theological perspective, and cultural context.[4] I think of the three realities in both physical and psychological as well as public and private terms. It is helpful to unpack Kelsey's three contextual categories to get a better picture of how contextual reality can significantly affect the process and outcome of the act of imagining:

- Exciting or boring, safe or dangerous, pleasurable or painful, etc.
- Doctrinal or traditional, faith-oriented or works-oriented, missional or attractional, etc.
- God-centered or self-centered, peaceful or rebellious, moderate or extreme, etc.

Kelsey locates the impact of contextual realities in the imaginative processes of remembering and anticipating. It's in our imagined memory of the past and hope for the future that context can make a big difference. We can see more clearly how a negative difference or bias enters into the picture with some examples of the imaginative processes of perception and interpretation:

3. Ibid., 41.
4. Kelsey, *Imagining Redemption*, 2.

1. Workplace amenities make it seem like a perfect place to work—or, boundary issues are ignored throughout the company.
   - How could these *concrete situations* affect one's imagined memory of the past or hope for the future?
2. Biblical equality is seen as the answer to all the problems in the church—or, dispensational theology disallows recognition by the church of certain spiritual gifts in modern times.
   - How could these *theological perspectives* affect one's imagined memory of the past or hope for the future?
3. Family gatherings have always been enjoyed by everyone throughout the family's history—or, family secrets dictate a culture of denial.
   - How could these *cultural contexts* affect one's imagined memory of the past or hope for the future?

Any of these cultural realities can bias one's imagination, by sugar coating on the one hand or falsifying on the other. We need a way to neutralize misrepresentation (misperception and misinterpretation) of meaning—in both directions!

SANCTIFIED IMAGINATION

This is where sanctified imagination comes in. Sanctification prevents situational, theological, and cultural misrepresentation. Sanctified imagination is not just a detached moment of reverie to manufacture comforting or exciting relief from the hazardous or humdrum ruts of life. It is an existential reality (not a fantasy) that redefines life as it is, whether good or bad.

Sanctified means, as I have stated earlier, bringing all imagery and visualizations under the lordship of Jesus Christ. It means lining up all our thoughts and prayers with Scripture and God's known character and thoughts for us—while framing pictures of his kingdom—in our spiritual mind's eye. Supporting biblical texts include:

PART II—Winning the War

> We demolish arguments and every pretension that sets itself up against the knowledge of God, and we take captive every thought to make it obedient to Christ.[5]

> Jesus declared, "I tell you the truth, no one can see the kingdom of God unless he is born again."[6]

> [I, Paul, pray] that the God of our Lord Jesus Christ, the Father of glory, may give to you the spirit of wisdom and revelation in the knowledge of Him, the eyes of your understanding being enlightened.[7]

Bruce Allen in his book *Gazing into Glory* shines a biblical light on the meaning of the mind's eye, a term also referred to by Bergen. Allen points out that this is what the Ephesians quote above is referring to. He also states that the word *mind* in the New Testament has two meanings. The first is imagination. Therefore, Matthew 22:37 can be paraphrased to read, "You shall love the Lord your God with all your heart, your soul, and your imagination."[8] The second meaning is to deliberate by reflection or meditation. Our mind's eye, then, is reasoning. Both meanings taken together define seeing through spiritual eyes.

Allen also points out that the word "enlightened" in Ephesians 1:18 "is the same word we derive the word photograph from. As the eyes . . . of our understanding or imagination begin to receive 'snapshots' of the Kingdom of God, we are made to see [through spiritual eyes]."[9] Then as we continue to practice framing pictures of the kingdom, with all our senses in play, we enter into a deeper, more meaningful and intimate walk with the Lord. Interestingly, this process is similar to the visualization technique used by athletes mentioned above—except that it is a lifestyle, not a technique!

---

5. 2 Cor 10:5.
6. John 3:3.
7. Eph 1:17–18, KJV.
8. Allen, *Gazing into Glory*, 87.
9. Ibid., 90.

INTEGRATING EMBODIED SIMULATION AND SANCTIFIED IMAGINATION

What steps do these two approaches take to turn meaning into action? I have inferred from Bergen's material the following three steps that are comparable to Allen's three steps:

1. Possibilities (Bergen, "Drawing Inferences")—making inferences about possibilities from the imagery and thoughts—imagined or real, abstract or concrete—regarding the reality of what has caught one's attention.
2. Opportunities (Bergen, "Creating the Subjective Experience of Understanding")—reusing one's brain systems to help create a subjective experience similar to a previous subjective experience of the best of the possibilities that offer the most promising opportunities.
3. Preparing for Action (Bergen, "Preparing to Act")—using the best opportunities for taking the most meaningful actions.[10]

Allen's three steps:

1. Visitation—in general, some form of the presence of the Father, the appearance of the Son, or the inner working of the Spirit. In every case, it is a manifestation—a breaking into our lives—of a living, caring, personalized, and responsive God:
    - It can be at any time or place.
    - It can be during peace or crisis.
    - It can be experienced individually or corporately.
    - It can be while reading Scripture or praying.
    - It can be while bowing down in worship or lifting up hands with praise.
    - It can be through hearing or healing.

---

10. Bergen, *Louder Than Words*, see esp. 244.

PART II—Winning the War

- It can be accompanied with a calming or a stirring of emotions, with a shout or a shiver.

  In every case it *focuses* one's attention on the presence of God and/or a call to follow Jesus with all of one's being and to consider all the possibilities that entails.

2. Revelation—guidance of the Holy Spirit primarily through searching Scripture and praying for insight into and confirmation of the opportunities that *connect* best with God's plan and purpose.

3. Activation—personal and/or corporate passion for intimacy with the Lord that *activates* a deeper and more meaningful walk with him.[11]

In other words, the Holy Spirit focuses our imagination and inspires us to connect with God's plan and purpose, so that we can activate a more intimate relationship with him. Now let's dig a little deeper into how this works with a biblical comparison and integration of some very important brain research with the Christian faith. It's not about science versus faith. It's not brain versus Bible! Not at all. It is about God: God creates and God initiates.

God is the Creator and Sustainer: "God created everything in the heavenly realms and on earth . . . , and he holds all creation together."[12] The very first thing we read in Scripture is that *God creates* the heavens and the earth and all its inhabitants. Note that he does so by speaking, and he continues to speak today:

- Through nature—"The heavens declare the glory of God; the skies proclaim the work of his hands. Day after day they pour forth speech."[13] "Their words aren't heard, their voices aren't recorded. But their silence fills the earth: unspoken truth is spoken everywhere."[14] "Since the creation of the world God's invisible qualities—his eternal power and divine na-

---

11. Allen, *Gazing into Glory*, see esp. 75, 129.
12. Col 1:16–17, NLT.
13. Ps 19:1–2.
14. Ps 19:3–4, MSG.

ture—have been clearly seen, being understood from what has been made."[15]

- Through human search for meaning—his word created what we are (our humanness), and continues to create, through what he has made within us, what we become (our meaningfulness).

We can conclude from this that when we look for meaning in our lives, we do well to look through spiritual eyes and stay close to God. He has created in us all we need to find *meaningfulness* in our lives, and he will continue to speak to us and guide us going forward—through both his written Word and the prompting and leading of the Holy Spirit. The bottom line for Christians is this: to see through spiritual eyes, we need both sight (perception) and *in*sight (interpretation). And both imagination ("the organ of meaning") and reason ("the natural organ of truth") need *super*natural *in*forming and *re*forming by the Holy Spirit. What we have then is a legitimate claim that we have God-given truth.

All this is beautifully expressed in a recent article written by Professor James K. A. Smith. In it he describes the process of developing a *biblical imagination* through the act of worship: "The Spirit *re*forms our imaginations by . . . inviting us to inhabit the rhythms of embodied, intentional Christian worship. God not only informs our intellects but retrains our heart's desires. Worship, then, is not just how we express what we already believe. It is also *formative*—an incubator for a biblical imagination."[16] Our God is indeed an awesome God.

So what about embodied simulation? As Christians, we find it offensive when God is marginalized and trivialized. But we must be careful not to throw the baby out with the bath water. Not all science is bad science. In fact, I find Benjamin Bergen's groundbreaking scientific research to be good science. He has done us a great service in providing objective observations of the intricate workings of the wonderfully made brains God has created in us.

15. Rom 1:20.
16. Smith, "Stop Blaming," 67.

I find it interesting that Bergen admits that the question remains open as to whether embodied simulation is sufficient for understanding or even necessary. I am arguing that it is incomplete. There is plenty of room for acknowledging that God created brain mechanisms involved in making meaning, and that he is existentially involved in supplying *true* meaning in the first place, prior to working it into the simulation process of accessing it and rehearsing it later. In other words, embodied simulation does not create the existence of true meaning, but it does create personal meaning (for better or worse) and make preexisting truth personally meaningful.

Two crucial points must be made. First, imagination governs the ability of simulation to do its job. In short, if you can't imagine the possibility of the existence of something, then you will not see it or perceive it as being meaningful. Embodied simulation in and of itself can create truth-for-me and also discover truth-for-everyone, or *true* truth. When imagination is unsanctified, however, it can easily be nothing more than postmodern solipsism. Arising out of the rejection of absolute, universal truth, it is the reduction of one's imagination to awareness of nothing but one's own personal experience. It puts one and one's personal meanings/truths at the center of the universe, versus God at the center of the universe and being the provider of universal truth for everyone.

When imagination is sanctified, the self-centered bias is removed and the door opens wide for the discovery and personal possession of universal truth. That is the saving grace and chief vehicle for meaningful memory work resulting in sanctified meaningful memories.

The second crucial point is that, in the act of creating, *God initiates* through the activity of the Holy Spirit. Again, this is where sanctified imagination comes in. Imagination plays by the same simulation rules as all other mental processes do. Therefore it is also a creative mental process. It creates personal meaning. Sanctified imagination, however, is not just a disembodied idea waiting around for us to come along and attach our own meanings to it, based on our personal thoughts and mental pictures and cognitive styles. Sanctified imagination is just as embodied as any other kind of imagination, but God is directly involved in the simulation. Imagination is sanctified when the Holy Spirit initiates and guides our reasoning.

The difference is that the person doing the imagining through simulation without sanctification creates the meaning. The person imagining through simulations *with* sanctification, however, does not create or even discover *true* meaning. True meaning is revealed through the simulation process *and* the guidance of the Holy Spirit. The bottom line is this: if you have Spirit-filled imagination, then you will have Spirit-formed, meaningful memories.

In terms of Allen's three stages for turning meaning into action, in combination with modified input from Bergen's three steps, a sanctified imagination/simulation process would look like this:

1. Focusing—on the presence of God and/or call to follow Jesus and to consider the resulting possibilities.
2. Connecting—with God's plan and purpose after guidance from the Holy Spirit for insight into and confirmation of the best opportunities.
3. Activating—a deeper and more meaningful walk with the Lord.

I see this as a balanced approach to making meaning. Actually, this chapter and book are both ultimately about seeing the work of God reflected in the world but also seeing God at work in the world and joining him. *World* has been appropriately defined as "the product of God's creation and the theatre of His manifest glory."[17] But the created world is a fallen world, and God is at work in that theater redeeming it, and manifesting his glory!

The question is, who is choosing to remain spiritually blind, because of their pride, self-deception, and/or lukewarmness—with a sealed-off imagination, unwilling to see through spiritual eyes what God is doing? Or who has spiritual eyes to see that are only half open, because they have sunk into a valley of pain filled with bereavement or besetting sin, depression, or defeat—or toxic memories? Or who

---

17. In Myers, *Eerdmans Bible Dictionary*, 1066.

Part II—Winning the War

is blessed with spiritual eyesight—eyes wide open—and wants, as disciples of Jesus, to receive the blessing Jesus refers to when, after thanking the Father for how he reveals the truth through the Son and his followers, he says to the disciples, "'Blessed are the eyes that see what you see!'"[18]—and that others do not see?

In closing, I recently found just the thing for all three categories of people. It is this wonderful prayer titled "The Valley of Vision," in a book of the same title of seventeenth-century Puritan prayers:

> The Valley of Vision
>
> Lord, high and holy, meek and lowly,
> Thou hast brought me to the valley of vision,
> > where I live in the depths but see thee in the heights;
> > hemmed in by mountains of sin I behold thy glory.
> Let me learn by paradox
> > that the way down is the way up,
> > that to be low is to be high,
> > that the broken heart is the healed heart,
> > that the contrite spirit is the rejoicing spirit,
> > that the repenting soul is the victorious soul,
> > that to have nothing is to possess all,
> > that to bear the cross is to wear the crown,
> > that to give is to receive,
> > that the valley is the place of vision.
> Lord, in the daytime stars can be seen from deepest wells,
> > and the deeper the wells the brighter thy stars shine;
> Let me find thy light in my darkness,
> > thy life in my death,
> > thy joy in my sorrow,
> > thy grace in my sin,
> > thy riches in my poverty,
> > thy glory in my valley.[19]

Amen.

18. Luke 10:23.
19. Bennett, *Valley of Vision*, x.

Afterword

I HAVE ATTEMPTED IN this book to address the unfortunate, commonly held, eyes-half-open view of spiritual reality. Many people have the mindset that *spiritual* is an abstract designation for either extraordinary or just plain weird. Further, its existence is seen as exclusively otherworldly, not down to earth; exceptional, never commonplace. There is no middle ground, where spiritual refers to various shades of light and darkness—good and evil—or of various "shades of gray."

My overriding concern has been to restore our understanding of spiritual reality to equal standing with all other forms of reality. As such, we can readily conceive of three distinct but overlapping worlds: physical, psychological, and spiritual (three different realities of things, thoughts, and a third dimension that makes sense of the other two). We can feel things with our hands and have thoughts and feelings about those things with our mind and emotions. But what do they mean, and are they true? This is where the spiritual dimension comes in. It's the glue that brings all other realities together into one unfragmented truth.

My goal has been to bring the spiritual realm into the very center of the discussion. We have our physical eyes and our mind's eye, and we are inexplicably drawn to bring the two together with our spiritual eyes. The three realities coexist every day, all the time.

Afterword

Therefore we need to have functioning spiritual eyes to properly apprehend each of these realities.

Scripture takes special note of seeing through spiritual eyes. For example, we read in the Old Testament that the prophet Elisha prayed to the Lord to open his servant's spiritual eyes so that he could see God's protective army.[1] We read in the New Testament that Jesus, as he approached Jerusalem, wept over the miseries that would befall Jerusalem after his rejection, and exclaimed, "If you, even you, had only known on this day what would bring peace—but now it is hidden from your eyes."[2]

I have applied the biblical concept of spiritual apprehension in the following ways:

- Recognizing objective results of demonic influence
- Redeeming church conflict by finding peace
- Substituting redemptive memories for toxic memories
- Trusting Spirit formation for spiritual well-being
- Translating sanctified imagination into meaningful memories

Throughout my forty-five-year academic and clinical/pastoral career I have endeavored to infuse my work with the thematic qualities of integration and compassion. *Integration* is evident in chapters 3 and 5, with the presentation of psychological coping mechanisms and demonic spiritual influences that coexist in church conflict, and the comparative analysis of three major approaches to making peace. It is also readily apparent in chapters 9 and 10, with the integration of brain science and biblical faith in making meaningful memories.

Compassion is clearly a driving force in chapters 4 and 6, which are built around biblical approaches to preventing memories that come back to haunt us and putting an end to toxic memories that stay with us and tear us down emotionally for years. In addition, chapters 7 and 8 provide an unwavering path from spiritual conflict to spiritual well-being.

1. See 2 Kgs 6:17.
2. Luke 19:42.

Afterword

Above all, I hope that through reading this book you will be more comfortable when you think about spiritual matters. In particular, I hope you will be able to acknowledge that Satan really exists and understand how he works—with *faith, not fear*. More importantly, I hope you will experience in your own life healing of the harm that Satan and his agents may have inflicted upon you.

When it comes to seeing and experiencing the spiritual reality of *healing, not harm*, the issue is light. Seeing through spiritual eyes is seeing the light through God's eyes: "In your light we see light."[3] In other words, we can truly see the good and evil in the world and in ourselves only when we see them through his eyes. Then and only then can we experience the ultimate outcome of good versus evil. That has been settled:

- *The Lord's plans for you are plans for spiritual well-being*:

    "I know the thoughts I think concerning you, says the Lord, thoughts of peace and not of hurt, to give you a future and a hope."[4]

- *He who is in you is greater than he who is in the world*:

    "You are of God—you belong to Him—and have [already] defeated *and* overcome them [the agents of antichrist], because He Who lives in you is greater (mightier) than he who is in the world."[5]

---

3. Ps 36:9.
4. Jer 29:11, Berkeley.
5. 1 John 4:4, AMP.

Appendix

Key Insights into Spiritual Warfare and Spiritual Welfare

ANALYSIS

I   *Satanic Influence Is Undeniable.*
  - The otherworldly mystery of spiritual conflict/warfare is brought down to earth by grounding it in real, objective human experience and verifying it biblically.

II   *We Are Fully Redeemed but Not Fully Sanctified.*
  - All evil attitudes, actions and memories must be brought under the lordship of Jesus Christ.
  - If we fail to fully sanctify our inner self, we open doors for evil spirits to enter and interact with our secret resentments and unresolved issues.

III   *We Act at Church Like We Act at Home.*
  - The emotional interface between individual families and the church family provides a potent context for the inevitability of church conflict.

Appendix

- The church becomes a receptacle for the displacement of unresolved family issues and dysfunctional patterns of behavior learned from the family.

IV *Satan Uses What We Give Him.*

- We mismanage and mask personal problems using a variety of psychological coping mechanisms, thereby falling into the trap of the devil, who takes us captive to do his will.
- Satan exploits and escalates our unsanctified attitudes and actions so that they become his—masked as ours.

V *Satan Uses Human Dynamics to Make Satanic Influence an Objective Reality.*

- If we wish to truly understand satanic influence as an objective reality, our first job is to establish the biblical reality or truth of what we are talking about.
- Our second job is to match the biblical reality of controlling spirits and their behavioral manifestations with the objective reality of mismanaged personal problems and their publicly verifiable psychological coping mechanisms.

RESPONSE

VI *All Conflicts and Sins Are Not Equal.*

- Moral equivalence marginalizes evil as an otherworldly metaphor rather than an objective reality in human affairs.
- Moral equivalence collects all conflicts and sins into a single category of undifferentiated sinfulness, which is a convenient but mistaken way of denying the presence of satanic influence.

VII *Reconciliation Is Not Unconditional.*
- Nowhere in the Bible is it suggested that we should dine with the devil by reconciling good and evil, God and Satan. Although forgiveness must be unconditional, restoring righteousness precedes reconciliation.
- Reconciliation and final peace cannot take place until forgiveness is given and received, sins are repented of and renounced, and justice is served.

VIII *Forget the Feelings but Not the Facts of the Painful Past.*
- Forget the emotional horrors of the past to release the possibilities for the future.
- Remember the factual wrongdoings, truthfully, in order to pursue justice and to shield against their recurrence.

IX *Sanctify the Inner Self and Renounce Sinful Ways.*
- Through prayer, the Holy Spirit will reveal the sinful themes of our attitudes and the hurtful extremes of our actions as well as counter the pain of our memories, and remove the stones—one at a time—from Satan's fortress (stronghold) in our inner self.
- Through prayer, the Lord will create in us a pure heart and renew a steadfast spirit within us, as we repent (regret) and renounce (reject) our sinful ways.

X *Redeem Toxic Memories.*
- If we wish to find lasting peace, we must put an end to those obsessive, self-imposed, random intrusions of traumatic thoughts and feelings that become a dreaded reality of existential permanence in our everyday life.
- We are bigger than our toxic memories, because we can reconstruct and reinterpret them, and we can filter them through sacred memories from redemptive biblical history to reactualize ourselves.

Appendix

XI *Develop a Long-Lasting Sense of Spiritual Well-Being.*

- Truly lasting peace cannot become a deeply rooted reality only through the preservation of the physical, psychological, and spiritual wholeness of our being, in the context of spiritual conflict.
- Truly lasting peace is a product of spiritual well-being—the holiness of our being, in the context of Spirit-formed Christlikeness.

XII *Create a Memory Bank of Sanctified, Meaningful Memories.*

- Peace that lasts is fortified by the intentional creation and accumulation of meaningful memories that undergird our spiritual well-being.
- Meaningful memories are sanctified when both imagination and reason are Spirit-formed by lining up personal imagery and visualizations with Scripture and framing pictures of the kingdom in the perception and interpretation of reality.
- If we cannot imagine spiritual possibilities, we cannot recognize spiritual realities and reason properly to create sanctified, meaningful memories.

Bibliography

Ackley, Alfred H. "He Lives." Homer A. Rodeheaver, 1933.
Allen, Bruce D. *Gazing into Glory: Every Believer's Birthright to Walk in the Supernatural*. Shippensburg, PA: Destiny Image, 2011.
Alonzo, Rebecca Nichols. *The Devil in Pew Number Seven*. Carol Stream, IL: Tyndale, 2012.
Barthel, Tara Klena, and David V. Edling. *Redeeming Church Conflicts: Turning Crisis into Compassion and Care*. Grand Rapids: Baker, 2012.
Bennett, Arthur, editor. *The Valley of Vision: A Collection of Puritan Prayers and Devotions*. Carlisle, PA: Banner of Truth Trust, 1975.
Bergen, Benjamin K. *Louder Than Words: The New Science of How the Mind Makes Meaning*. New York: Basic Books, 2012.
Crosby, Fanny J. "Blessed Assurance." Word Music, 1986.
———, "Praise Him! Praise Him!" (1869).
———, "To God Be the Glory." Integrity's Hosanna! Music and Word Music, 1997.
Farnsworth, Kirk E. *Integrating Psychology and Theology: Elbows Together but Hearts Apart*. Washington, DC: University Press of America, 1981.
———. *When the Bride Is Attacked: Find Peace in the Midst of Spiritual Warfare*. Lake Mary, FL: Creation House, 2010.
———. *Wholehearted Integration: Harmonizing Psychology and Christianity Through Word and Deed*. Grand Rapids: Baker, 1985.
Farnsworth, Kirk E., and Rosie Farnsworth. *All Churches Great and Small: 60 Ideas for Improving Your Church's Ministry*. Valley Forge, PA: Judson, 2005.
Frangipane, Francis. *A House United: How Christ-Centered Unity Can End Church Division*. Grand Rapids: Chosen, 2005.
Friedman, Edwin H. *Generation to Generation: Family Process in Church and Synagogue*. New York: Guilford, 1985.
Greenfield, Guy. *The Wounded Minister: Healing from and Preventing Personal Attacks*. Grand Rapids: Baker, 2001.

Bibliography

Harrington, Ken, and Jeanne Harrington. *Deliverance from Toxic Memories: Weapons to Overcome Destructive Thought Patterns in Your Life.* Shippensburg, PA: Destiny Image, 2013.

Harris, R. Laird. "Proverbs." In *The Wycliffe Bible Commentary*, edited by C. F. Pfeiffer et al., 553–83. Chicago: Moody, 1962.

Hawkins, Greg L., et al., *Reveal: Where Are You?* Barrington, IL: Willow, 2007.

Jackson, John Paul. *Unmasking the Jezebel Spirit.* North Sutton, NH: Streams, 2002.

Jamieson, Robert, et al., *Commentary on the Holy Bible: A Commentary, Critical and Explanatory, on the Old and New Testaments*, 176. Grand Rapids: Zondervan, 1934.

Jeeves, Malcolm. *Minds, Brains, Souls and Gods: A Conversation on Faith, Psychology, and Neuroscience.* Downers Grove, IL: InterVarsity, 2013.

Jones, E. Stanley. *A Song of Ascents: A Spiritual Autobiography.* Nashville: Abingdon, 1968.

———. *Victory through Surrender.* Nashville: Abingdon, 1966.

Kelsey, David H. *Imagining Redemption.* Louisville: Westminster John Knox, 2005.

Lemmel, Helen H. "Turn Your Eyes upon Jesus." Singspiration Music, 1922.

Lewis, C. S. "Bluspels and Flalansferes: A Semantic Nightmare." In *Selected Literary Essays*, edited by Walter Hooper, 251–65. Cambridge: Cambridge University Press, 1969.

———, "Is Theology Poetry?" In *Essay Collection and Other Short Pieces*, edited by Lesley Walmsley, 22. London: HarperCollins, 2000.

Morgan, G. Campbell. *A First Century Message to Twentieth Century Christians.* New York: Revell, 1902.

Myers, Allen C., editor. *The Eerdmans Bible Dictionary.* Grand Rapids: Eerdmans, 1987.

Peterson, Eugene H. *A Long Obedience in the Same Direction: Discipleship in an Instant Society.* Downers Grove, IL: InterVarsity, 2000.

Pickett, Fuschia. *The Next Move of God.* Orlando, FL: Creation House, 1994.

Putman, Jim, et al., *Real-Life Discipleship Training Manual: Equipping Disciples Who Make Disciples.* Colorado Springs, CO: NavPress, 2010.

Sande, Ken. *The Peacemaker: A Biblical Guide to Resolving Personal Conflict.* 3rd ed. Grand Rapids: Baker, 2005.

Smedes, Lewis B. *Forgive and Forget: Healing the Hurts We Don't Deserve.* New York: HarperOne, 1996.

Smith, James K. A. "A Whirlwind Take on Culture." *Christianity Today* 57/10 (2013) 65–67.

Ten Elshof, Gregg A. *I Told Me So: Self-Deception and the Christian Life.* Grand Rapids: Eerdmans, 2009.

Volf, Miroslav. *The End of Memory: Remembering Rightly in a Violent World.* Grand Rapids: Eerdmans, 2006.

———. *Exclusion and Embrace: A Theological Exploration of Identity, Otherness, and Reconciliation.* Nashville: Abingdon, 1996.

Bibliography

Ward, Michael. "How Lewis Lit the Way: Why the Path to Reasonable Faith Begins with Story and Imagination." *Christianity Today* 57/9 (2013) 36–41.

Watson, George D. *Soul Food*. Cincinnati: Knapp, 1896.

White, John, and Ken Blue. *Church Discipline That Heals: Putting Costly Love into Action*. Downers Grove, IL: InterVarsity, 1985.

White, Tom. *Breaking Strongholds: How Spiritual Warfare Sets Captives Free*. Ann Arbor, MI: Servant, 1993.

Willard, Dallas. *The Divine Conspiracy: Rediscovering Our Hidden Life in God*. San Francisco: HarperSanFrancisco, 1998.

www.ingramcontent.com/pod-product-compliance
Lightning Source LLC
Chambersburg PA
CBHW070927160426
43193CB00011B/1601